SMALL FLY
TECHNIQUES

THE LYONS PRESS
Guilford, Connecticut
An imprint of The Globe Pequot Press

SMALL FLY
TECHNIQUES

LARRY TULLIS

THE LYONS PRESS
Guilford, Connecticut
An imprint of The Globe Pequot

The Lyons Press is an imprint of The Globe Pequot Press.

10 9 8 7 6 5 4 3 2 1

Printed in The United States of America

Color photographs by Larry Tullis

Illustrated by Rod Walinchus

ISBN: 1-58574-810-2

The Library in Congress Cataloging-in-Publication Data is available on file.

Frontispiece: Don Vose Casting a dry fly, Provo, Utah.

CONTENTS

OVERLEAF: *Lefty with a nice cutthroat on the Green River, Utah.*

LEFTY'S PREFACE

One of the great joys in my life has been sharing fly-fishing knowledge with old and new friends. When I think about my old friends, the fishing pros of my generation with whom I often fished over the years, and from whom I learned so much, I am reminded of General MacArthur's famous line that "old soldiers never die, they just fade away." I hope this is true of old fly-fishing professionals, too. Several of them, including Joe Brooks, Al McClane, Harry Kime, and Les Eichorn, aren't around for me to go fishing with anymore. But they enriched my life in so many ways. In fact, their life's work left something wonderful for all of us to enjoy. So I like to think that like old soldiers, old fishing pros don't die, they just pass from the scene for a little while.

But some of the "old professionals" from my generation are still really active. England's John Goddard is now 70 years old, but he's still going strong, writing books and sharing his vast knowledge with others. George Harvey, the best American trout fisherman I have ever fished with, is now in his 80s, but you'd never know it the way George prowls the streams dropping #22 flies to sipping trout. Then there is Charley Waterman, who has been my favorite fishing writer for many decades; Australia's Rod Harrison, a walking library of fishing information who should be considered one of that country's national treasures; and

Dave Whitlock, Nick Lyons, Gary Borger, Al Troth, George Griffith, and a host of others.

The thing that distinguishes the lives of these fellows, I think, is that aside from being great human beings and enjoyable streamside companions, each of them is giving something of value back to this great sport of fly fishing — whether it's a piece of writing, a fishing technique, a fly pattern, or just the influence of his character on his contemporaries — that is being passed on to our new generation of fly-fishing pros, and will continue to endure and be passed on to future fly-fishing generations.

This passing of the mantle of knowledge and love of the sport from one generation to the next, with each generation adding new understandings and refinements before passing it along again, is one of the finest aspects of our fly-fishing heritage. Which brings me to the book you have before you.

Fly fishing is better than ever today, and a major reason for this is all the great work our new generation of fly-fishing pros is doing. In saltwater, I think immediately of Dan Blanton, Nick Curcione, Ed Jaworowski, Bob Popovics, Lou Tabory, Jon Cave, and Mike Wolverton. When I think of fly fishing in our eastern freshwaters, I think of John Randolph, Tom Rosenbauer, Charley Meck, and Bob Clouser. Western fly-fishing pros that come to mind are Dave Hughes, Dave Engerbretson, Mike Fong, Jim Teeny, Trey Combs, and the author of this book, Larry Tullis.

In *Fly Fishing for Trout*, I wrote the following:

> But trout are now being fished hard in most places in the world, and they seem to have become more educated. So that now, especially in calmer and clearer waters, the angler needs to more closely

match with his imitation the natural insects that are hatching. Nowhere is this more obvious than in the western part of the United States. The trout that inhabit our western streams today are tougher and much more difficult to deceive, and western fly fishermen are having to develop all sorts of sophisticated techniques to fool wise trout. This is contrary to the myth (often repeated by trout fishermen in the eastern United States) that the best and most refined trout fishermen are in the East! But the truth of the matter is that most of the refinements being made in trout fishing, at least today, are being made by fly fishermen on our western waters.

I wrote these words before I ever met Larry Tullis. And he wrote his book before he had ever read this passage I just quoted above. So I'm not recommending Larry's book to you because he agrees with me. Although I have to confess it doesn't bother me that he does!

I first met Larry when he guided me last year on the Green River in Utah. I was most impressed with his competence and knowledge of trout fishing, particularly his views on how trout — particularly the catch-and-release trout that so many of us are fishing over today — are becoming accustomed to the presence and pressure man has brought into their environment; how they are adapting to that pressure by becoming very selective in their food choices; and how the highest measure of success in fly fishing for trout in the future will be achieved only by those anglers who are willing also to adapt, to change their technique and learn how to fish small flies effectively. I told Larry he ought to write a book about this, and he agreed to do so.

I think Larry's small fly thesis (which of course, you can judge for yourself), that the primary adjustment that selective trout are making is to reject the commonly fished medium-sized flies in favor of small ones, is a sound argument. And an understanding of what Larry has to say about small flies for trout, together with the small fly techniques he recommends — particularly the use of a two-fly indicator rig — are well worth the money you have spent for this book and the time I hope you will spend reading it.

Although Larry has contributed articles and photographs (he is also a superb outdoor photographer) to a number of fly-fishing magazines over the last few years, this is his premier appearance in book form, and I am pleased to present it to you as the third volume on trout in Lefty's Little Library of Fly Fishing. Thank you.

Bernard "Lefty" Kreh
Cockeysville, Maryland

INTRODUCTION

Since fly fishing began, it has been changing. Despite the illusion that the sport is tradition-oriented, nearly every aspect of fly fishing is constantly evolving. The sport is undergoing a metamorphosis regarding tackle specifications, techniques, philosophy, fly design, types of water fished, and kinds of species fished for. And the trout themselves have changed, primarily due, I think, to their increased interaction with humans. But even though there has been and always will be change, there are also the fly-fishing constants or truths that cannot be ignored just because other aspects of the sport change. This book is about those changes and constants, and how to blend them together not only to understand trout better, but to catch more of them.

So what do small flies have to do with these changes and these constants, and why should you bother to learn more about fishing small flies? I think there are three principal reasons.

First of all, fly fishermen should begin to accept the fact that moderate to hard-fished waters are the norm in trout fishing today. Even in remote areas of Alaska, trout can feel the pressure from anglers that fly or jet-boat into areas where trout are known to congregate.

Also, regrettably, on most occasions fly fishing is no longer a sport of solitude. At streamside today, even though for a little while we may be able to focus on the biosphere swirling around our legs and enjoy some private time with the trout, it likely won't last long. Soon there are apt to be other anglers on the river.

Finally, with catch-and-release fishing becoming the rule rather than the exception today, trout in all habitats — particularly those who have undergone the stressful experience of being impaled on a sharp hook, pushed and pulled around their living quarters, and then subjected to the humiliation of being pulled out of the water and handled, fondled and photographed by some unseen force — are going to change and adapt their behavior to avoid such stress in the future.

But fortunately, trout have a strong sense of survival, and except where man has neglected conservation practices or polluted the water beyond the trout's survivable limits, they have adapted well to the presence of man.

But adapt they have. And adapt they will continue to do. And as they adapt to the presence of humans, trout become more *selective,* first by keying in on foods that are generally safer than others — safer because they are plentiful, easy for the fish to identify accurately, and easy for them to reach without having to expose themselves to predators. That fact is really the major premise of this book: *in the trout's habitat, safe foods generally equal small foods.* That's not to say that trout won't eat large foods on occasion, but as a rule, when fishing pressure increases, trout key in on smaller foods most of the time. At these times, the *size of the imitative fly pattern and how it's presented become critical.*

Although trout are often referred to as being "wily" or "smart," the reality is that they have brains the size of a pea. They do not have the ability to absorb large amounts of information, analyze it, and make a conscious choice from that body of information. But the reason that trout constantly frustrate and make fools of fly fishermen (that hopefully have much bigger brains) is that they have a marvelous set of instincts. This is best demonstrated in their vital feeding behavior. While trout cannot analyze a complex set of variables as humans can, what they can do is to keep zooming their focus in until they weed out all but one or two of the principal features or characteristics of the food. Then they can act quickly on that simple amount of information.

On mayflies, for example, trout may regulate their feeding behavior by concentrating on the insect's wings that they see in their cone of vision first; on grasshoppers it may be the legs that hang under the surface; on minnows it may be the eye of the baitfish. Trout feeding on eggs in clear water often get very selective just on the color of the egg. Other trout will ignore almost everything but the drift. This type of fish may take a hundred different fly patterns if drifted properly, but none if the drift is improper. Do you see what I'm saying? This is why trout often seem so focused and so selective regarding the size of an imitation, while completely ignoring — or at least not being bothered by — the big hook sticking from the fly's abdomen. Your job is to figure out what are the principal characteristics of the food supply that the trout are keyed in on at the moment and offer them an imitative pattern that possesses those characteristics. It's really not that hard, as I hope I can show you.

And keep this in mind. When trout key in on small flies, they must also increase the number of grabs per ounce of food. That means that with small fly techniques you will not only fool selective trout more often, but you will also have many more chances to have your fly intercepted by a hungry trout.

As I will be discussing in more detail later in the book, "educated" trout have now become very suspicious of medium-sized flies. So many anglers who were once considered experts are now often frustrated because their old techniques don't work well anymore. It's generally not because there are fewer fish or more fishermen, it's because the trout have changed and the anglers did not change with them.

Who can fish small flies? Anyone can. But most anglers simply refuse to fish the small fly patterns that best imitate small foods. There are a number of reasons for this, I suppose. Many people don't use small flies because they are under the impression that small flies are difficult to fish, or because they think big fish won't take small flies. That is simply not the case anymore — particularly with the new presentation techniques and the stronger and finer tippets that have been developed, coupled with the way in which trout in heavily fished waters are changing their habits in response to fishing pressure.

As a veteran fly-fishing guide, I have seen everyone learn how to use small flies, even guys that had a hard time seeing their shoes, much less a #22 Griffith's Gnat. In fact, one blind client of mine even performed well by concentrating on sounds and the feel of tension on his line. There is simply no reason for anyone to be scared of small flies. Techniques will be discussed to offset any excuse such as "bad eyesight," "can't get the leader through the eye," "can't land a big fish on a small fly," or "small flies don't catch big fish."

Nearly all types of trout water have applications for small flies. Lakes, ponds, sloughs, small streams, large rivers and spring drainages all have times when small flies work well. Two exceptions might be extra large lakes and oceans where the trout follow baitfish in open water.

These are usually difficult fishing waters for the fly rodder anyway. Leave those fish for the trollers. The third exception might be anadromous trout, such as steelhead or sea-run browns, whose behavioral habits parallel salmon more than trout, but even these species prefer smaller patterns on occasion.

The term "small flies" requires parameters. I like to think of all flies tied on #16 or smaller hooks as small flies. However, if a fly pattern has a larger size range of, say, #14 to #4, as grasshopper patterns do, then I regard the lower third of that size range (#14 to #12) as "small flies." Micro-streamers and similar patterns are also developing a devoted following. Other small flies include varieties of terrestrial insects, which are incredibly effective on some streams, even during a hatch. Being able to master the techniques of fishing the natural hatches of such small insects as Tricos, Blue-Winged Olives and micro-caddis will make you feel like a pro!

To catch trout consistently on small flies, you must understand something about the foods they eat. You do not need to have a Ph.D. in entomology to catch trout, but you should learn the basics about the types of foods trout eat. Scientific terms will not be used in this book unless they are also the terms commonly used by fly fishermen. Actually, the common insect names, that in terms of color or pattern describe what the insect most looks like, are often more accurate and better descriptions for fishing purposes anyway. An example is the Blue-Winged Olive. Most fly rodders know what that mayfly is, but there are actually at least nine species of this *Baetis* that can all be imitated with one pattern tied in several sizes. It would take an expert with a microscope to identify the exact species, but that scientific knowledge would probably not help him catch any more fish than the guy who just knows that it is a mayfly with an olive body. This book, then, is written by an angler for anglers, to help you catch more trout, in more situations, by understanding trout and their feeding habits better.

All types of trout foods are important if trout feed on them. We cannot ignore foods just because they do not fit into the "classic four" insect groups (mayfly, caddis, midge, stonefly), because hunger and exact imitation are not the only considerations in choosing a fly pattern. There are reasons, for example, why attractor and suggestive flies sometimes outproduce exact imitations. To assist you in becoming a more effective small fly fisherman, we will consider the main things that will increase success. First — and most important — is the proper technique, followed by an understanding of trout behavior, an understanding of trout foods, and finally, knowing how and why to choose the right small fly pattern and how to present it properly in the various fishing situations you can expect to encounter.

If you are excited about the possibility of learning how to catch trout on small flies, then you are already thinking like a small fly angler. Fishing small flies is fun, intriguing and often even entrancing. Once you learn a few tricks it is even easy, but most of all it's productive. You would probably be surprised at the size of fish that regularly feed on minute edibles. Believe me, the "big fly, big fish" rule does not always apply, especially when trout get selective due to the kind of fishing pressure that trout waters are experiencing today.

To overcome the numerous misunderstandings that exist about small fly fishing, along with an examination of small fly patterns and the small fly techniques that have been developed over the last decade or so, is what this book is all about.

I believe that small flies are the future of fly fishing for trout. I also believe that once you learn the basics of fishing small flies, you will catch more trout, in more kinds of waters, in more adverse situations, than you ever did before. In fact, I'm willing to guarantee it.

OVERLEAF: *Selective spring creek rainbows.*

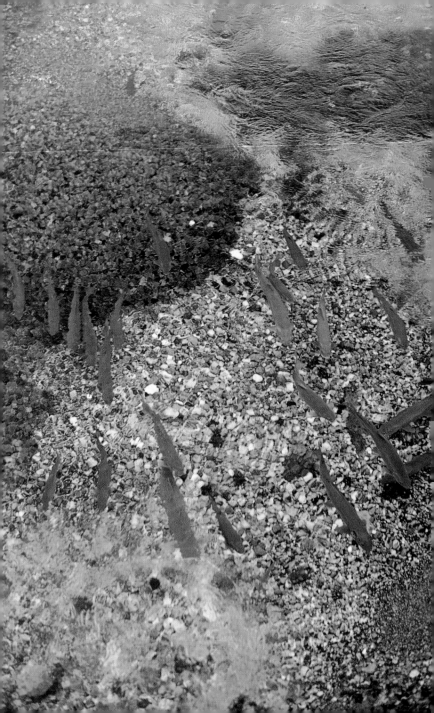

CHAPTER ONE

TROUT FEEDING BEHAVIOR AND ITS RELATIONSHIP TO SMALL FLY FISHING

FEEDING BEHAVIOR CLASSIFICATIONS

Whether you're on a familiar local stream or on strange water you've never fished before, an understanding of trout feeding behavior is important because it will help you to recognize exactly what the trout have been doing, and then be able to make a prediction as to what they will likely be doing next, at the time when you make your presentation. If you know why trout do certain things, then you can capitalize on that behavior. Although these things relate most directly to the small fly techniques I will be discussing, they can also be readily applied to all types of fly fishing.

There are many variations of the feeding behavior and lifestyle that trout exhibit as a result of their interaction with humans. I divide trout behavior into three categories: that of *the uneducated trout*, *the educated trout* and *the catch-and-release trout*. There can be many subdivisions or combinations of these three categories, of course, but for simplicity's sake, these are the ones that I have found to be helpful in reaching a better understanding of trout behavior. Try to relate these categories to each of the waters that you regularly fish. Or if you are going to new water, try to find out in advance from other anglers which category would best describe the fish in that watershed, and you will be able to prepare (at least mentally), for the type of fishing techniques you'll likely need to use there.

Uneducated Trout

Uneducated trout are those that receive little or no fishing pressure during the year and seldom even see a human predator. These trout react to stimuli the way nature has dictated for thousands of years. Food, procreation and shelter from predators are the only things they require, and therefore seek, throughout their lifetimes. Much of their feeding activity is totally uninhibited and is seldom selective. Any selective behavior that they may seemingly demonstrate can probably be attributed to the predominance of one particular food type in their habitat, so that the trout simply don't need to feed on anything else. Also, in many places where uneducated trout exist, food may be scarce or competition for it so intense that the fish will frequently pounce with vigor on almost any food offered to them.

High country lakes and streams, wilderness areas and innocuous watersheds are the common homes of such uneducated trout. Some also exist in large lakes and saltwater environments that see little fishing pressure per surface acre in a year. These will likely be wild fish. Or they may sometimes be hatchery fish that for some reason or another have been undisturbed and unfished for a time.

This type of fish generally spooks easily and is not likely to feed again until it feels safe. And when it does resume feeding freely, an accurate imitation of the prevalent hatch may actually not be very effective. Instead, put something out there that catches its eye. Attractor flies, such as Royal Wulffs, Humpys, or Zug Bugs, are perfect because they catch the trout's eye quickly. And because this category of fish has not narrowed its focus down to one or two characteristics of an insect or bait that it wants to feed upon, anything that looks edible and will fit into its mouth is food. For example, such fish often get extremely excited by a fly pattern being dragged across the current, something selective fish seldom do.

Educated Trout

Educated trout are those that have been fished over considerably in habitats where many trout are landed and kept by anglers. In this type environment, "stupid" fish don't last long and the fish that survive have somehow keyed in on foods that they consider to be "safe." Does that ring a bell? It should say "small flies" to you. In such habitats, other trout may feed only at night or during twilight hours, or occasionally on large meals, such as frogs or smaller fish, to narrow their window of vulnerability while keeping their feeding time to an absolute minimum. These will often be the biggest trout in the watershed because they have continually eluded capture. Medium-sized flies can be totally ineffective with such fish, because insects of this size have long ago been discarded from their daily menu.

In this habitat, moreover, some trout naturally run for cover when threatened. And some are very wary from having been hooked before but having escaped by breaking off the angler's line on roots, rocks, or aquatic vegetation. These type of fish are spooky. Wading slowly and quietly is always the rule with them. Some situations even require that the angler kneel down or crawl to within casting distance to keep the trout from being alerted to his existence. In clear water, long casts with long, light leaders are needed, as are accurate casts, because these fish will normally not stray far from their chosen feeding lanes. And as you might imagine, a fly drifting unnaturally is suspect and will usually be avoided or rejected.

In backcountry areas such as the Chilean Andes or Canada's north country, trout are fished for only in certain seasons. Through the winter, when food is scarce and the water cold, these trout lose some of their natural defenses. But the spring thaw brings a feeding binge when they are often as dumb as their uneducated cousins. With fishing pressure, however, they quickly revert back to their cautious selves. In these areas there may frequently exist a mixture of uneducated and educated trout. Resident fish in such heavily fished spots will be harder to fool than their cousins that are migrating through the watershed to spawn or feed.

Areas with closed fishing seasons see the same phenomena. Opening day usually sees lots of fishing action and lots of fishing pressure. The trout that are not harvested right away quickly revert back to their cautious ways. The fishing slows and most seasonal anglers lose interest. But the small fly angler can experience great action throughout the season in this type water.

Catch-and-Release Trout

The third class of trout are those that are caught and released. The feeding behavior of this category of trout has not been documented until recently. But we are learning that with the proliferation in recent years of catch-and-release or slot limit waters, trout actually get used to the presence of man, and include man in their concept of natural habitat. This often produces some odd behavior. This category is growing quickly and is one that anglers should acquaint themselves with if they intend to fish on C & R (catch-and-release) waters.

In the more popular C & R waters, trout are often fished over constantly, of course. If they spooked every time a human presence was detected, they would likely starve to death. Their sense of survival won't let them do that, if at all avoidable, so each trout gradually starts to adapt its feeding habits to deal one way or the other with the human presence. This creates a very complex set of variables that often frustrates fly rodders, because each trout is doing something different. Just remember that the fish are not so much cunning as they are simply keyed in on one or two of the behavioral characteristics of their food supply. If you will discover what characteristics the majority of fish are keyed in on, you will most certainly experience a high rate of success.

It is very rewarding to stand in one spot and discover what every fish around you is feeding on. I used to think that some fish were just too smart to catch, but the more I fish the more I think that every feeding fish (and even some that are not feeding) can be caught with the right combination of technique and fly pattern.

C & R trout will often keep right on feeding when a human presence is detected. But they will automatically go on increased guard. The angling ideal, of course, is to be stealthy enough to approach the fish without them knowing it; but with these fish it is not often necessary. Many C & R trout can be approached to within 10 feet by a careful wader. Some anglers use a monocular to watch individual fish feed to discover what they are feeding on, then tie on an imitative pattern that closely matches the natural. This is exciting fishing, much like hunting because you spot your prey, study its habits, plan your tactics, and then make your move.

On my home waters of the Green River (in Utah, below Flaming Gorge Dam) some trout have been caught so many times that they even seem to know that release is imminent! After hook-up, many of these fish make an initial rush with much head shaking, but then come into hand docilely with little resistance. It's almost as if they were saying, "Come on buddy, I know the routine, let me go now so I can get back to feeding." Other trout may be used to being hooked but deal with it by fighting very aggressively in hopes of loosening the hook or breaking off. One 21-inch trout from the Green River took me 20 minutes to land and when I did, I discovered it had eight other flies in its mouth, including three flies of the same size and pattern (obviously tied by the same person). Another particular fish I caught three times in 20 minutes. The point is that unlike uneducated trout that may quit feeding for a day or more after being caught, C & R trout will usually go right back to feeding. One 25-inch Snake River finespot cutthroat trout on the Green River was caught 40 times in one season just by my clients and the clients of three other guides that work on the Green with me. Some fish on the Green were surely caught as much as 80 or more times in one year! That's a real testament to catch-and-release fishing, but as I've said, each catch-and-release trout has developed its own particular response to fishing pressure, and it can produce some very odd feeding and fighting behavior at times.

One type of behavior that is becoming more and more common on C & R waters is that the fish are learning that wading anglers kick up lots of food. These trout will actually follow anglers around, feeding on the nymphs, scuds and other aquatic foods that the angler has dislodged with his boots. Some anglers have capitalized on that fact by fishing at their feet. Besides not being very sporting, these anglers who are purposely kicking up gravel to attract trout are also creating a disturbed biological seal in the streambed which will take years to heal and return to its natural state. You may have heard of this practice, called the "San Juan Shuffle." Fortunately it has been outlawed in many places, and rightly so. If you find trout following you around, simply back out of the water. Heck, most anglers wade too much anyway, standing exactly where they should be fishing.

Small flies were made for shallow water. Most anglers would be surprised to learn what a huge number of trout regularly feed in just 3 to 18 inches of water. Since shallow-water trout in C & R waters are not easily spooked by a relatively cautious angler, you can often get very close to such trout and observe their feeding behavior.

When I guided on the Henry's Fork in Idaho, Harriman State Park ("the Ranch" as it's long been known) was an intimidating and intriguing place for many anglers. For some, this was the first time that they ever fished over catch-and-release oriented trout. I talked to numerous old timers there who lamented the loss of the good old days on the Ranch when the fishing was much better than it is now. Of course, what had happened here was that the fish had changed their behavior, but many of the old timers had not. But the thoughtful fly fishermen at the Ranch who were willing to change their fishing technique to respond to the change in the trout's behavior continued to do very well.

Some of the biggest trout in the Ranch were bank feeders. They positioned themselves on the current edges in shallow water to feed. A sloppy cast often put them down or made them even more selective. The fly had to be presented to the fish before the line or leader, because the trout would stop feeding immediately when they saw a leader track or felt a fly line impact nearby on the water. Anyone that presented dry flies in the traditional up-and-across method only caught a few of the smaller trout. In yet another example of adapting technique to changes in trout behavior, many successful anglers began fishing instead with a down-and-across technique. This technique is now commonly used to present dry flies to bank feeders in many places on the Ranch, but just 10 or 15 years ago it was almost unheard of.

FEEDING BEHAVIOR CHARACTERISTICS

Selective trout are intriguing because each trout develops slightly different habits. In a pod of six feeding fish, you may encounter six different types of feeding behavior. One feeds on scuds grubbed from the aquatic vegetation, one on drifting nymphs along the bottom, one on ascending midge pupae, one on midges suspended under the surface film, one on emerging midges, and the last one alternates between the adult midges and scuds missed by the grubbing trout. Three look like they are rising to adults, when in reality only one is, and then only part of the time. The others are actually feeding on other stages in the insect's life cycle, or at different levels in the water column — the drift levels — in which the insects are moving or being transported along by the current.

Then add to that mixture the habits of the individual fish, the multiplicity of foods available in the watershed, hydrological variances (current speed, water depths, etc.), the daily atmospheric changes that affect trout and the hatches, variances in light intensity, water temperature and fishing pressure, and you can begin to see the thousands of variables and permutations that are influencing your fishing. No wonder we sometimes don't catch fish!

Faced with such a daunting challenge, many people just resort to the "chuck and chance" method, tying on one pattern after another until they find one that seems to work better. Despite getting an occasional hook-up, they end up wasting the better part of a day fooling around haphazardly with these thousands of variables without ever really finding out what's going on.

The 10 percent of the fishermen that catch 90 percent of the trout have something in common. They have all learned to respond to hints that would indicate *trout feeding behavior at that particular time and place*. And I would venture to say that 100 percent of those 10 percent expert anglers can and do fish small flies when the situation requires small flies, as it frequently does.

But let's take the "daunt" out of "daunting." In learning to deal with fish feeding behavior, you are not required to absorb, sort, analyze and figure out every single piece of fishing data everywhere. You are simply required to intelligently respond to hints you receive through your own streamside observations and awareness of the success (or failure) of other anglers around you. But you cannot respond to these hints if you don't know what you're seeing. With that said, let's examine the most important aspects of trout feeding behavior.

Strike Zones

Strike zones are one of the least understood aspects of trout behavior. Predicting the size of strike zones, as well as how and when fish feed, have been pastimes for fly fishermen since the sport began. Still, no one has come up with a consistent method. Bass and walleye seem to vary their feeding habits in some respects in conjunction with the phases of the moon. From what I've seen, trout don't usually have the same lunar feeding schedules. Light intensity, seasonal changes, weather changes, food migrations, fishing pressure, water temperature, water clarity, water type and pH potential, etc., all seem to affect the trout's daily feeding schedule and the size of the strike zone in which it will be feeding. So don't try to predict feeding behavior, just deal with it as it comes.

When you can see that trout are using a large strike zone, cover lots of water with your fly and have fun with the aggressive trout who are willing to travel to your fly from a distance. If the strike zone is small, zoom your own focus into just trying to bump the fish in the nose with your fly and take satisfaction in your successes. Let what you observe about strike zones determine, at least in part, what kind of presentation you use.

Drift Levels

Let's discuss drift level as it relates to feeding behavior. As trout key in on various insects (or the same species of insect in different stages of its life cycle), the level in the water column in which an imitative fly drifts becomes critically important. Most people just think "deep" or "surface," "nymph" or "dry fly." But selectively feeding trout have the ability to choose among many more subtle but very precise categories of drift level than that. For example, an individual trout, depending upon its feeding behavior — and, of course, that behavior can change numerous times throughout the day — has the option of keying on the drift levels of ascending insects, suspended insects, emerging insects, newly emerged adults, egg-laying adults or spent adults — six levels of drift. And all of these can exist within one inch of the surface!

Spawning Behavior

As it is in humans, sexual behavior is another strong drive behind the variations in the behavior of trout. Something I learned from bass fishing is that gamefish exhibit three types of feeding behavior associated with their spawning activity — pre-spawning, spawning and post-spawning. And, I'd like to add a fourth, which I call "spawning groupie" behavior.

Trout in their pre-spawning stage have a lot of latent energy. At this time, they may go on energetic feeding binges and sometimes they are quite aggressive and will attack large streamers with a vengeance, more out of nervous tension than out of hunger, I think. This often happens when the fish are enroute to their spawning grounds. Once they arrive at the general spawning area, they usually slip into some deep water ahead or behind the actual spawning substrate and sit waiting for the right time to start their spawn, still exhibiting a good deal of that nervous tension. Trout in this condition sometimes have a very small strike zone and need to be bumped in the nose. Your fly invading and disturbing their privacy is often met with a quick grab that again seems to be more out of nervous tension than of actual hunger.

As the spawn commences, the trout group up and begin to pair off. The female begins digging the nest by fanning the gravel, while the male stands guard to chase away intruders. At this time, the male is particularly susceptible to streamers because he is aggressively defending the nest. The female, on the other hand, is not as aggressive but is more of a fastidious housekeeper. As she digs the nest, she often catches things drifting into her nest and crushes them in her mouth. Eggs are of special concern to her and her mate, because eggs from other nests may contaminate their own. This activity often appears to be feeding behavior, but during the actual spawning activity, few fish feed. The salmon fishermen among you will recognize that there are many parallels between the behavior of trout and salmon during the spawning period.

Post-spawn trout often stay in the general vicinity of the nest for several weeks. As the spawning urge diminishes, their hunger returns and is often robust. Many feed heavily on the eggs and nymphs kicked up by other fish that are still spawning. At this time, eggs are an important source of energy for trout and they will sometimes feed on eggs to the exclusion of all other food.

"Spawning groupies" are not actually spawning fish, but are wandering fish that have been attracted by spawning activity or the food it is producing. Actually, such non-spawning fish often greatly outnumber the spawning fish in a spawning area. They suck up the nutritious eggs and nymphs kicked up by spawners, sometimes with reckless abandon, but at other times with a good deal of selectivity. The eggs may be from other trout, or as is the case in Alaska, from salmon or other spawning species.

Some anglers have an attitude toward egg imitations and refuse to use them, regarding their use as inappropriate or substandard fly fishing. That attitude is quickly changing, however, as anglers realize that the modern definition of fly fishing — which I think is entirely reasonable and ethical — includes imitating all types of natural trout food. Alaskan-style trout fishing has gone a long way toward fostering this change in thinking, I think. More and more, the fly fisherman is beginning to understand that at those times when the trout are feeding heavily on eggs, foregoing the use of imitative egg patterns is like tying both hands behind his back. There are times when trout will absolutely ignore anything but eggs, and fishing an egg fly can mean the difference between a fishless or a fantastic day.

The traditionalists who refuse to fish egg patterns advance the argument that fishing for spawning fish (or in spawning areas) is biologically unsound, because it disturbs spawning activity. Two points are important to remember in this regard. First, most of the fish in spawning areas are not spawners but are actually post-spawners or groupies. It has been estimated that the number of non-spawning fish in a spawning area may be as high as from 50 to 95 percent! And secondly, even the spawning fish that are hooked, played, and released properly are affected little by angling because they are so keyed into spawning activities that they exclude almost all other considerations from their lifestyle. They simply go right back to spawning. That is especially true with the trout in catch-and-release areas that have probably been caught and released before anyway.

However, that does not mean an angler should not exercise caution and follow sound environmental practices when fishing a spawning area. The one thing that can do irreparable damage to spawning efforts is wading on the spawning beds themselves. This crushes hundreds of eggs and displaces the trout from where they want to be. Anglers need to recognize spawning beds, spawning areas, and spawning seasons, so that even if they choose not to fish for spawning trout, at least they won't be accidentally causing severe damage. I'm constantly amazed, and disappointed, at the number of fly fishermen that ignorantly tromp all over spawning beds. And ignorance is no excuse. Oval-shaped depressions of clean gravel in riffles almost always denote spawning activity.

As in other situations where fish feel pressured, spawning area feeders start to key in on certain things. The drift of the egg fly is first, its color second, and its size third. *Note that this is different from the trout's feeding behavior when they are concentrating on insects,* for then size is far more important than color. This behavioral characteristic is important for the small fly angler to keep in mind, because with increasing fishing pressure during spawning seasons there comes a natural increase in selectivity. The big, gaudy-colored egg patterns that were once thought to be effective will largely be ignored. Small, accurately sized and properly colored eggs are the patterns of choice. The most important characteristic of fishing an egg fly — how it drifts through the water column — will be discussed later in the techniques chapter of this book.

At those times when many anglers are fishing egg imitations, the trout may decide to key in on a "safer" food, and will turn to the small nymphs that are dislodged from the streambed by other spawning fish in the area.

In Alaska, though, the abundance of salmon eggs, possibly coupled with the relative lack of available nymphs, often dictates that the trout feed 100 percent on eggs until the fall season begins, at which time the eggs become less prevalent in the watershed.

Curiosity

Curiosity often initiates a non-hunger feeding response from trout. Since a trout's survival depends on its ability to adapt to its environment, it is constantly sampling new foods as its natural response to finding them in its biosphere. If this were not so, trout would never adapt to areas where foods were of an uncommon variety. Trout eat the Pancora crabs in South America, shad in large reservoirs, and crayfish in certain watersheds. Hatchery trout consume meal pellets that are thrown to them in the hatchery and then later switch to whatever happens to be the most available natural food in the water in which they are eventually stocked. Therefore, it stands to reason, I think, that even selective trout will also sample or "test" new small foods.

In experimenting with various fly patterns, I discovered that some trout who would reject most standard fly patterns were absolute suckers for small, strangely colored flies. For example, in heavily fished waters, Pheasant Tail Nymphs tied in purple, orange, black, bleached pheasant, olive, or chartreuse often outproduced the standard dressings of this pattern.

Everyone knows the effectiveness of attractor dry flies at certain times. Even selective fish will go out of their way to take an attractor dry fly in the right conditions. Think about it: if you had been eating only green peas, one at a time, day after day, you'd be ready for a change of diet, too! Similarly, if a trout gets "bored" with its mechanical feeding behavior, out of curiosity it will often pounce on an attractor pattern tossed in its general direction.

Regarding attractor patterns, I have found also that larger patterns seemed always to be automatically rejected by the fish; but small attractor patterns produced well, even though such small attractor patterns were quite different from anything the fish would normally see in their environment. I think that simply because these patterns were different, and because they were within the proper size range, they captured the trout's attention and were accepted and curiously tested. Trout don't always respond to such outlandish tricks, of course, but when they are being finicky on normal foods, you might consider throwing them a curveball. It may give you an advantage.

Flashback Nymphs are similarly effective. Flashbacks are basically standard nymph patterns, such as a Pheasant

Tail, Hare's Ear or Biot Nymph, to which have been added a silver, gold or pearlescent Mylar wingcase in place of the original. This may imitate the air bubble present in some emerging nymphs. But I think it more often just catches the trout's eye and triggers its curiosity.

The best attractors are flies which trigger something inside a trout to make it change its feeding habits. Nobody knows why that is, but the popular attractor patterns, Wulffs, Trudes, Madame Xs, etc., can be deadly at times. A Royal Wulff tied on #16 to #20 hooks is always a good bet, even when there is a hatch going. Small peacock-body nymph patterns, such as the Prince or Zug Bug, also get aggressive hits at times.

Few fly fishermen fish attractor patterns in small sizes, but they ought to, because they work amazingly well. Attractors are also some of the best patterns for getting fish to rise during non-hatch periods.

If you have seen a fish zoom up to your fly two or three times, you can be sure that at least you've captured its curiosity. Gary LaFontaine once told me about some trout that got more and more excited as he dropped his fly on the water, briefly, several times. On his first cast, when the fly hit the water the fish acted as if they were thinking, "What was that?" Then on the second cast, the fish acted as if they were thinking, "There it is again." On the third cast they were waiting for it and attacked it with a vengeance. Gary confirmed this strange behavior by having a companion view what was happening from underwater. Curiosity had churned the fish into a frenzy.

Largemouth bass are known for their curiosity towards odd food offerings, but I believe trout have an equal amount of curiosity for smaller flies.

A double on magnificent browns who were fooled by a midge. ▶

Conditioned Response

Trout learn things much the same way dogs did in Pavlov's experiments to demonstrate conditioned response. You will recall the Russian physiologist conducted experiments in which he rang a bell every time he was about to feed his dogs. The dogs soon learned that the bell meant food, but perhaps more importantly, they began to salivate in anticipation of the food to come. It was a physical, measurable response to repeated stimuli. We all know now that a repeated procedure can become part of the mental and physical conditioning of animals that lack the capacity of memory and the ability to recall the past like humans. The trout animal has the same ability, and can have its behavior altered by repeated stimuli.

If trout get caught and released by flies attached to leaders that are visible (and all are, I believe), they soon learn through conditioned response and negative reinforcement that leaders are to be avoided. Their response to the appearance of a leader on the water can be to discontinue feeding for a short time, at least until the physical evidence that triggered those responses is removed from their mental input. That amount of time generally ends up being long enough for your fly to pass on by the fishes' strike zone, untouched. The obvious solution, when you suspect this is happening to you, is to fish down and across, so the fly approaches the fish before the leader and line.

Unnatural fly drag — particularly the insidious "microdrag" that I will discuss later — is another easily recognized mental input for trout. Selective, educated and C & R trout have become conditioned to automatically reject any possible food source that is drifting improperly. *Drag is the single most important consideration — far ahead of fly size or color — when fishing for selective trout.*

And this is particularly true with nymphs. While most anglers concentrate on achieving drag-free drifts with their dry-fly patterns, they usually (and mistakenly) give less thought to the effects of drag on a nymph pattern. Since surface and deeper currents vary, mending and maintaining an appropriate amount of slack and angle of presentation are absolutely critical components to successful nymph fishing. You even need to estimate the distance upstream from your primary target (the fish) that you will need to cast your fly line to allow sufficient time for the nymph to sink to the proper depth in the water column where the trout is on station. *All things considered, compared to dry flies, nymphs are more difficult flies to use in fishing for selective trout; but, on the other hand, they are also more productive, if you do it right.*

Trout even become conditioned to fly patterns that are used frequently. That's why every year someone comes up with a new, hot fly pattern. The fish have become quite used to the standard patterns — they have learned they are not "safe" anymore. Showing the fish something a little different often turns the key on their conditioned response mechanism. So experimenting with fly patterns that are different than those everyone else is fishing can very often have good results.

Also, many, many anglers — for reasons I have never been able to figure out — insist upon using imitative patterns that are bigger than their natural models. These people reach a stream and without any sort of well-reasoned game plan immediately begin casting out a medium-sized fly, such as a #12 Adams, a #14 Humpy, or a #10 nymph. If tying flaws exist in the pattern, at these larger sizes they are much easier to detect. But more importantly, so many people fish the medium sizes that the trout quickly become conditioned to rejecting these sizes first. I believe that if you will use patterns a size or two smaller than usual, your success will increase.

Another conditioned response feeding habit that is little understood is what I like to call "parallels." During a hatch, trout will feed heavily and constantly on a particular insect that is plentiful in their environment, and the characteristics of that insect food become imprinted on their minds through conditioned response. When the hatch ends and the insect is no longer available, the trout switch to another food source, yet the insect's conditioned imprint remains with the fish for a month or two. During that time, while trout will seldom take an exact imitation of the earlier hatch, an attractor pattern which contains characteristics similar or parallel to that of the earlier hatch insect may trigger a feeding response.

Most attractor flies are thought of as unscientific and therefore are rejected by "sophisticated" anglers. Actually, attractor flies are flies that have proven over time that they possess certain triggers for trout. Remember that trout are unable to key in quickly on perhaps no more than one physical characteristic of their food supply. If that characteristic is the upright wings of a mayfly, for example, the trout may have their feeding response triggered by the white wings of a Royal Wulff, even though they are presently feeding on a plentiful supply of caddisflies.

So, when fishing attractor flies, think "parallel." Ask yourself what insect the trout were feeding on one month ago and use an attractor fly that has similar but enhanced characteristics. Examples include white-winged, Trude-type flies which will work well one month after the trout have fed on stonefly adults and midges. Similarly, parachute dry flies with white calf's tail or Z-Lon wings are deadly during and after a mayfly hatch. Prince Nymphs work well after the scud or stonefly seasons, even when the trout are feeding predominantly on dry flies. Rubber-leg flies work well if trout have seen lots of bugs with thick legs, such as hoppers, stoneflies, beetles and cicadas.

Good attractor fly patterns normally contain a number of the following triggering characteristics: white upright or Trude-style wings; a bit of Crystal Flash in a wing or in other parts of the fly body; brown or grizzly hackle; peacock herl bodies which have a special iridescence that can trigger a feeding response even from the most selective hatch feeder; rubber legs which twitch enticingly, and so on. One of my favorite attractor patterns is a small rubber-leg nymph or dry fly. They are almost impossible to find in fly shops, but the trout love them.

In fact, small attractor-type flies are the most overlooked flies around. Small (#16 to #20) attractor patterns such as Royal Wulff, Lime Trude, Z-Lon Parachute, and Humpy dry flies, as well as Prince, Flashback, Rubber-Leg, Zug Bug, and Hare's Ear nymphs, will often work well on selective trout, even right in the middle of the hatch of an insect that really has none of the exact characteristics of these particular patterns. Because even though these imitative patterns are quite different than the naturals the fish are currently feeding on, such attractors possess the magic feeding triggers that were created by imprinting from a previous hatch or food source.

Obviously, the attractor patterns are also popular for non-selective fish and for searching the water during non-hatch periods, due to parallel triggers, curiosity, or just plain old-fashioned hunger.

Another trigger is the "think fast" response, similar to what your reaction would be if someone threw a baseball toward you and said, "Think fast." Trout will sometimes respond to foods that come into their strike zone quickly. Apparently, the fish suddenly become aware of something approaching them, and without hesitation, either dodge it altogether or suck it into their mouths, just as you would either dodge or attempt to catch the baseball. Streamers are natural choices for this kind of fishing, but nymphs or wet flies swung in front of a trout can also trigger such a response. Although it is more of a natural response than a conditioned response, this "think fast" or "baseball" response will sometimes trigger trout that are normally being selective and finicky during feeding time on a hatch of naturals.

Perception Factors

Here is an important question to think about. If a trout takes your perfect imitation of an emerging mayfly, mistaking it for a midge or an ant, is it then "exact imitation?" The fish was still hooked but not for your reasons. Just as fishing attractor flies may be more of a science than most anglers think, fishing exact imitations may often be less. Because in the end, the only thing that really matters is the trout's perception of your fly.

Sometimes it is better to let the trout decide what it wants to eat, rather than you trying to make the decision for it. Which brings us to the subject of suggestive fly patterns. The Hare's Ear is a perfect example of an excellent suggestive pattern. It imitates nothing in particular but many things in general. It could be any one of dozens of mayfly nymphs, cased caddis, scuds, sowbugs, midges, stoneflies, snails, craneflies or other aquatic larvae. Greased up and fished in the surface film (in small sizes) it works very well to suggest various emergers, spent adults, or even terrestrial insects such as ants, beetles, jassids or micro-hoppers.

Suggestive patterns include many fly patterns that are generally considered attractor flies and are often not used by match-the-hatch "experts." But in small sizes they become excellent search patterns to help you observe and key in on the feeding patterns of trout.

In recommending that you take the time to understand the value of attractor and suggestive fly patterns, I'm not trying to take away from the science of matching the hatch. In fact, I hope I'm helping you to understand hatch matching better. When you can determine what a particular pod of fish is feeding on, then obviously, matching the hatch is the best way to go. But think back over your own fishing experiences. What percentage of the time that you have spent in fly fishing for trout have you actually had the opportunity to match the hatch? I'll bet it's less than 50 percent of the time — and for some anglers it may be a much lower percentage than that. So how are you going to have successful fishing during half or even more of your stream time when there is no hatch available to match? I think the answer is the thoughtful use of attractor and suggestive fly patterns.

Also, when you are fishing new water or have not yet found out what the trout are feeding on, then the use of attractor or suggestive patterns is often the best way to start your fishing day. Once you land a fish or two, using a stomach pump for a bit of streamside forensic pathology, or becoming aware of other clues, such as what kind of water you caught your first fish in, or at what depth, or at what time of day, or in what sort of light conditions, etc., you may be able to zoom your focus down to more specific imitations or places to fish.

This is system fishing. Most anglers simply keep tying on fly patterns in random order until they start catching trout and will probably waste most of their day in doing so. They will seldom tie on small flies, either because of a lack of faith that the fish are even feeding, or from the erroneous belief that if bigger flies won't catch fish then small flies won't either. Using a system of good search patterns with attractor and suggestive flies, and analyzing what you learn from observation, can get you into more fish and in much less time.

Using this criteria, there is really no distinct line between attractor, suggestive, and exact imitations. The trout must be considered the final expert as to how it perceives the fly. If you tell the fish that you want it to feed on Pale Morning Duns when all day long it's taking caddis larvae and scuds, then I don't care how well you match the Pale Morning Dun hatch. You aren't going to catch that fish!

But perhaps, just perhaps, a suggestive pattern like a Hare's Ear or an Adams will often get the action started, and then you can go from there. What have you got to lose? You have already found out that presenting Pale Morning Duns was a waste of time.

I know it often frustrates anglers when they think they know exactly what the trout should be feeding on, but are having only marginal success. But starting out with a broader range of view, utilizing a fishing system of trial and error and searching, and then refining your fly pattern and presentation techniques once you get some input from the fish, is much more effective.

UNDERSTANDING FLY REJECTION

All of the trout behavior I have been discussing relates to using both small and large flies. If you will keep this behavior in mind while you're on the stream, your success will improve, or at least you will better understand what you are observing. For example, when trout are visible, watching their reaction to your fly is extremely educational. I am lucky enough to have fished the Green River in Utah for almost 1,000 days, and much of what I have learned about trout behavior was gathered on that water as I observed the great Green River trout and their reactions to my flies. And what I learned on the Green I have had confirmed many times in all the other trout waters I have fished.

Here's what I know about this important matter of fly rejection. A rejection is when the trout starts toward your fly, or otherwise acknowledges its existence, and then turns away before taking it. If a trout rejects your fly, it should tell you something. Trout have poor distance vision, but as they get close to the fly, they can see it quite clearly. And when they get close to the fly and reject it, there are many reasons.

However, there are quite a few common rejection mysteries that can easily be solved with a little observation and recognition.

Leader drag is one of the most common of all presentation flaws and the principal reason for fly rejection. As I discussed earlier in reference to conditioned response, selective trout, especially those found in C & R waters, have seen so many dragging flies that when they see a fly doing something different than the other naturals on the water, it immediately triggers a conditioned response and an automatic rejection.

On the other hand, fly drag can be desirable in some waters, but not in most heavily fished waters where catch-and-release fishing is prevalent. When I was in Chile recently, the brown trout would seldom take naturally drifted flies. These fish wanted their nymphs, emergers, streamers and even dry flies to be dragging across the current, and they wanted exaggerated retrieves. So although most selective trout like natural presentations, it is important to know that at some times and places you can fish more effectively with a dragging technique.

Another reason for rejection is fly size. Selective feeders do not measure your fly with a micrometer to see if it is the right length, but they do get an ideal fly size imprinted on their minds from their constant feeding on naturals. An exact imitation one or two sizes too big looks grossly out of proportion next to the other naturals. If you get rejections, drop down in fly size and try to improve your natural drift.

If you are matching the hatch and are still getting rejections, it often means that the trout are simply feeding on a different life-form stage of that same insect. If they reject your dry fly but still appear to be feeding on the surface, it is a likely assumption that they are feeding on emergers and not the duns.

The rise-form of the trout can tell you a lot about what the trout are feeding on, even if you have not yet had an opportunity to examine the hatch. An aggressive, splashy rise often means the trout are feeding on caddis. A gentle rise that leaves a bubble often means the trout are on mayflies. A dimple on the surface or dorsal fins that break the surface without leaving a bubble indicate feeding activity on emergers or midges. An occasional boil along a bank usually means stoneflies or grasshoppers. These guidelines are not always accurate, but they are a good place to start.

Another reason for fly rejection can be that your fly gets lost in a raft of the naturals. If there are thousands of small insects on the water, as occurs with some mayfly, midge and micro-caddis hatches, and you are using an exact imitation of the naturals, it is likely getting lost in the raft of naturals. Why would the trout take your fly over the thousands of naturals that are on the water? The leader track attached to your fly certainly does not help either.

When this situation occurs, try a different pattern, such as a white-wing parachute dry fly, a Trude, a small Royal Wulff, a Humpy or an Adams, in a size similar to the naturals on the water. The fact that the pattern is slightly different may catch the fish's eye. Once you have its attention, if the drift is natural looking, the size right, and you have put the fly in its feeding lane, your chances of hooking the fish are pretty good. Natural looking imitations are best fished in moderate to sparse hatches, rather than in blanket hatches where your fly will likely get lost in the crowd.

OVERLEAF: *Blanket hatch on holes at Can-O-Worms, a section on the Green River, Utah.*

CHAPTER TWO

UNDERSTANDING TROUT FOODS

FOOD BASICS

If you don't understand what trout eat, it will be pretty difficult to imitate those foods. A basic understanding of trout foods is necessary to better understand what fly should be used at a given time and place. If you are presenting dry flies to trout that are feeding on emergers, I can assure you won't do very well. For our purposes, while we will not be getting too entomological, we need to examine the various stages of insect metamorphosis and how to go about imitating them. There's just no getting around it: *to be a successful trout fly fisherman, you must acquire a basic knowledge of trout foods.*

Trout will initially concentrate on foods that are plentiful and large, but as we have discussed, when fishing pressure increases they turn to feeding on smaller insects. But then they must eat more small insects to equal the same calorie count they were realizing from bigger foods, and this, in turn, results in more feeding attempts by the fish and more catching chances for the angler.

During a hatch, the trout do not necessarily feed in any uniform manner, nor on the same life cycle stages of an insect. They will usually start on nymphs when the nymphs begin moving, then go to emergers as the insects start rising to the surface. As the hatch becomes thicker, the trout may switch to newly hatched adults or perhaps even egg-laying adults or dead and dying adults.

But it is important to note that not all trout will alter their feeding preferences as insects in the hatch go through their various life-form changes. Some trout will feed exclusively on nymphs, while others will only start feeding at later life-form stages, when other feeding fish in the neighborhood have stimulated their feeding response.

Besides aquatic insects, scuds and sowbugs are often very important foods, especially in the winter and spring when they may be the trout's most abundant food source. Aquatic red worms are important in some areas, too, especially in many of the tailwater fisheries in the West.

Knowing the type of insect that is hatching is much more important to the fly fisherman than knowing its exact species. Exact species often can only be identified by experts with microscopes. All you need to know is that it's a mayfly, caddis etc., as well as its size, color, and perhaps the life-form stage the fish appear to be feeding on most. Watch the clues and with a little practice, you can easily identify which foods the trout are keying in on.

Each insect has life-form stages that can be imitated. For example, a caddis has six life-form stages, including larva, pupa, emerger, emerged adult, egg-laying adult and dead or spent-adult. For each of these stages, there is an imitation that will work.

It's really not very complicated, especially if you will keep in mind that some fly patterns, such as suggestive patterns, imitate more than one insect or more than one life-form stage of an insect. Some people really enjoy getting into entomology and learning to imitate every stage of every insect, while others concentrate more on presentation and less on fly patterns. Both approaches can work well. The ultimate ideal of fly fishing, of course, is to have an effective pattern and an ideal presentation.

Few anglers take time out to study the insects in the stream or lake where they are fishing. But if you will set your rod aside for a few minutes and closely examine the rocks, aquatic vegetation and water surface, you will learn some interesting things about the insects and crustaceans in the area you are fishing. There are several ways to go about examining trout foods.

Just turning over a few rocks and examining the underside will give you an idea of what nymphs are around. Pulling up a handful of aquatic vegetation or a sunken stick usually uncovers hundreds of aquatic insects. Look closely at the current edges, scum lines, and back eddies where adult or spent insects have been washed by the current. Check shoreline vegetation for resting insects. Watch the places where the fish are, and try to locate some feeding fish for clues as to what insects, and at what life-form stages, they are feeding on.

A window screen stapled to two sticks makes an excellent sample collector. Stretch it out in the current and allow drifting insects to collect against the screen for a few minutes, then raise it and examine the densities of various insect types. If one is predominant, it will probably be the one the trout are feeding on. A small, aquarium-style net is very valuable for scooping adult and emerging insects from the water surface. You will usually find that a large proportion of the insects in any given stretch of water will match a #16 or smaller hook. So if you use a screen to collect insects, make sure that the mesh is not so large that it will allow the small bugs to pass through.

Or, after you have caught a trout, you can use a stomach pump to see what it has eaten. Stomach pumps need to be used with care, of course, so you do not damage the trout. Stealing a trout's breakfast in this manner may seem a little cruel, but if done properly, it does not hurt the fish and is very educational. It is obviously a way to know with absolute certainty what fish are eating.

These moments of observation and sample collection are often the most valuable time you can spend on trout water. You can keep the collected samples in a small glass bottle to match later, or at streamside compare your own fly patterns to the naturals to determine how closely their size, shape, and color match.

Another valuable tool for this work is a small booklet that Gary Borger has published called the *Borger Color System* that allows you to match the insect's size and color accurately.* Keep in mind that insects quickly change color once they are removed from their natural habitat.

MAYFLIES

Mayfly adults are distinguished by their upright wings that give them the appearance of a small sailboat. The mayfly nymph often has gills along its abdomen and two or three tails. It can live in all types of trout water, from rapids to stillwater. Mayflies start life as an egg. The nymphs grow until they get ready to hatch, at which time they swim to the surface where they drift for a short distance while they break through the rubbery surface tension of the water. Their wing pad cracks open and they begin to emerge from their nymphal shuck. The mayfly's wings are crumpled at first, but as they finish emerging,

---

*Available from Gary Borger Enterprises, P.O. Box 1745, Wausau, WI 54402, Telephone: 715-842-9879.

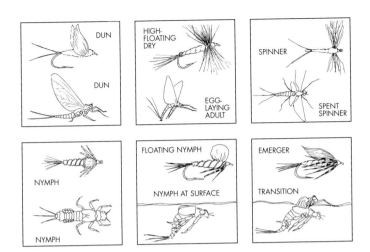

Mayfly Life-forms (below) & Imitative Patterns (above)

fluid pumps into the wings until they are upright and ready for flight. The adults that emerge, called duns, first stand on the surface tension without sinking, but then fly to streamside vegetation as soon as possible to complete their metamorphosis. There they shed another skin and only then are they sexually mature. At this stage they are referred to as spinners. Spinners mate in airborne swarms, and then the females flutter along the surface, depositing eggs. When done, the spinners die and drift with their wings outstretched on the water. Not all mayflies complete their life cycle. Some emerging mayflies — called stillborn duns — die. Others are crippled and cannot fly away.

Most mayflies hatch during the spring through the fall. Few hatch during the winter, though some winter hatches can occur on tailwater fisheries and spring creeks.

Every stage of the mayfly, excepting the egg, can be imitated and fished. See the illustration above for examples of the various stages and pattern types for each.

Mayfly nymphs are usually best fished along the bottom, but as a hatch begins, the trout will follow the nymphs up through the water column and feed on them at whatever level the trout find most productive and easy.

In riffle water, trout will usually stay on the bottom, then rise to the ascending nymphs. But in slower currents the trout will often suspend themselves just a few inches under the surface and feed just under or right at the surface. Fish suspended in this manner often key in on only one life-form stage. Some trout key in on the ascending nymphs, some on the insects at the surface film, some on the emerging duns, and some on the duns that are still trailing their nymphal cases.

When fish are feeding on mayfly duns, you will usually see a bubble in the rise-form rings. When trout feed on other life-form stages of the mayfly, they may break the surface but they won't leave a bubble.

There are many fly patterns that imitate mayflies — it has been the most imitated of all insects since fly fishing began. The larger mayfly species always receive the most attention in the fly-fishing press, but day in, day out, the small species are the most prolific and the most valuable. Pale Morning Duns, Blue-Winged Olives, and Tricos are extremely ubiquitous, existing in many trout streams throughout the world.

MIDGES

Midges are much more abundant than any of the other insects found on most trout streams, and often hatch year-round. Yet, oddly enough, midges are one of the least imitated of all the aquatic insects. I think that the reason must surely be that because of their small size, many fly

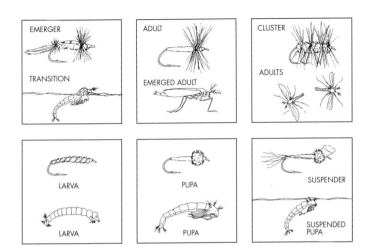

Midge Life-forms (below) & Imitative Patterns (above)

fishermen consider midges difficult to fish and not as important as they really are.

Midges look like mosquitos, but usually have wings that are shorter than their bodies. The two wings lay flat over the body or are slightly V-shaped. They may have visible, fuzzy antennae. From the egg stage the larva — which looks like a tiny worm — grows in aquatic vegetation. Unlike the mayfly, midges have a complete metamorphosis, which means they have a pupal stage between the larval and adult stages. The pupal stage rises to the surface where it hangs vertically in the surface film for a distance while it breaks through. Once through the film, the adult emerges, still trailing its larval shuck, and drifts for a while before taking to flight. The adults mate, then the females deposit their eggs on the water and die. This egg-laying stage often triggers trout feeding activity that causes some small, splashy rises, but the other stages are more important as a food source for trout.

A large midge is imitated with a #12 hook, but most imitations are tied in small sizes (#18 to #24). Even in these small sizes, surprisingly large trout feed on them regularly, because of their availability in vast numbers. Even 20-inch trout regularly feed on midges.

The trout get into a steady feeding pace on midges and because of the length of time the midge stays on the water, the trout can feed with a slow, deliberate rise that causes only a small dimple on the surface from a rise-form. Sometimes the rises are so gentle you might think your eyes are playing tricks on you.

As with most aquatic insects, there is a natural drift of midge larvae twice a day, even when they are not prepared to hatch. When the hatch is heavy, midges will often clump together into small rafts of insects, and to conserve energy the trout will gorge themselves on these clusters of midges instead of bothering with single insects.

Something to remember is that because the midges are small, the trout will need to consume vast quantities to become satiated, so you can have many chances to catch a midge-feeding trout. But since these trout will not expend lots of energy nor move a great distance when feeding on midges, your presentation must be accurate and natural.

If you encounter a situation where you're making an offering to large, selective trout, midges will give you an advantage because they are on the trout's list of "safe" foods and may trigger an automatic feeding response.

Small cranefly species are often mistaken for midges, so they can be imitated with the same flies. Because midges and small craneflies can hatch every day of the year, the trout become conditioned to feeding on them when other foods are scarce. If larger insects, such as mayflies or caddis, begin their hatch, the trout often switch to them.

  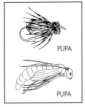 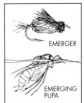

  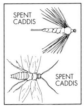

Caddis Life-forms (below) & Imitative Patterns (above)

But if daily stomach samples were taken from trout throughout the year, midges would be found in more abundance than any other insect.

CADDIS

Caddis are moth-like insects that have tent-shaped wings. From the egg, caddis larvae hatch and grow in many environments. There are three types of caddis larvae. One — called a cased caddis — builds a case of sand or vegetation fragments. Another variety is the grub-like free-roaming caddis which does not build a case. The third type spins a delicate net on the stream bottom and lives there. As caddis prepare to hatch, they change into their pupal stage and swim rapidly to the surface. They are the best swimmers of the typical insects that trout feed upon. Once at the surface, they quickly break through the surface film, emerge, and fly away. The whole emerging process at the surface can occur in less than a second. Once mated, the females flutter over the surface, laying eggs, then die with wings outstretched. One type of caddis adult actually dives back underwater to lay its eggs.

Some caddis hatch in the spring or the fall but most occur in mid-summer. They may hatch any time of day, but evening caddis fishing can often be very productive.

Because caddis pupae are fast, trout must intercept them very quickly so they don't get away. The result is a rise-form that is splashy and erratic. Splashy rises are a good sign that caddis are present. When such rise-forms are identified, you can also be sure a large number of trout are feeding on the ascending pupae, so at that time pupa, emerging pupa, and adult caddis imitations will all usually take trout.

(Incidentally, this phenomenon occurs with other aquatic insects that you may identify fish feeding on. If one stage of imitation does not produce sufficiently, try a pattern that imitates a different stage.)

While many trout prefer naturally drifted midges and mayflies, caddis patterns are often fished with some action to imitate their fast-swimming or egg-laying antics. Caddis adults can be skittered on the surface — especially in fast water — or naturally drifted with the current. Caddis larvae are best drifted naturally, but the caddis pupae can be swung in the current to imitate swimming motion. In fact, in many streams and lakes, it is frequently more productive to imitate the pupal stage of the caddis than the adult stage.

Micro-caddis, that seldom exceed 5 mm in length, exist in many streams and many midge type patterns are taken for these caddis. These patterns can be fished as you would fish midge imitations, but sometimes the flies can be swung in the current.

STONEFLIES

Stoneflies have a great size variance. Most fly rodders know about the various large patterns such as Salmon Flies, Golden Stones or Large Brown Stoneflies, though smaller patterns can be very important at times. Stoneflies have long, oval-shaped wings that are held flat over their back. The nymphs have two tails and a distinctly segmented body with segmented wing pads. Unlike mayflies, their gills are under their chest. They only exist in clean, well-oxygenated streams.

Stoneflies live from one to five years as a nymph before crawling to shore to emerge as adults. The adults mate, then the females flutter over the water depositing eggs, then die. Because they crawl to shore to hatch, there are no emerger patterns for stoneflies, just nymph, adult, and spent-adult life-forms. To find out if stoneflies are hatching, look around the stems and underside of leaves of shoreline vegetation to see if they are there. The winter varieties are often seen resting right on the snow. If you come across an insect hatch in winter or early summer that you cannot identify, there is a good chance that it is a small stonefly hatch.

The small species of stoneflies have nymphs that look similar to mayfly nymphs, and imitations of one will serve for the other. I frequently like to use small-sized rubber-leg nymphs when I think the trout are feeding on small stonefly nymphs.

Big adult stoneflies cause the trout to make large boils in the water surface when feeding, but the smaller and spent adults often trigger a very subtle rise-form — in fact, the trout may barely dimple the water surface, as with midges. But occasionally they will create a medium-sized boil, similar to a mayfly rise-form.

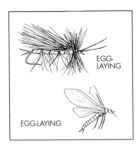 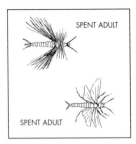

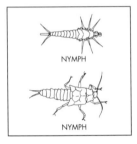 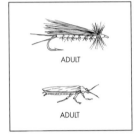

Stonefly Life-forms (below) & Imitative Patterns (above)

I recall one late June day while fishing the stonefly hatches on the Copper River in Alaska. There were many larger Brown and Golden Stones hatching, but at the tail of one pool, a number of big rainbows were feeding on something I could not identify right away. The large stonefly patterns I had been using were ignored here, so I kept reducing my fly size until I was fishing a #16 Elk-Hair Caddis. A 22-inch rainbow took my fly, and after a lengthy battle I landed it and noticed that its gullet was overflowing with small brown, black, and bright yellow stonefly adults. There were at least five species of stonefly adults on the water that day, in addition to caddis and a few mayflies. But the 16 to 24-inch trout in that area were keyed in on the small stoneflies, which were the most abundant fly at the time.

CRUSTACEANS

Common crustaceans include scuds, sowbugs, crayfish, and the tiny daphnia. Even though they are extremely important in the trout's food chain, only occasionally are crustaceans imitated by anglers, probably because they are not insects. They should be, though, because they are a highly nutritious food source for trout, and are common, even prolific, in many streams and lakes. On Utah's Green River, for example, a recent study showed that there were over 1,000 scuds per square yard of stream bottom. On the Colorado River below Lake Powell, scuds are the primary food source for most trout.

Scuds — Scuds are small, shrimp-like crustaceans that exist in many trout lakes and streams. Scuds are heavily segmented and flattened laterally with many legs and antennae sticking out of their underside. They grow up to 1 inch long but most have a body length of from 1/2 to 1/8-inch. They exist in various colors; the most common are gray, amber, tan, olive and brown. When scuds die they often turn an amber/orange color.

In streams, scuds are best fished as a nymph, on a natural drift. In lakes, they swim erratically, so a short, jerky retrieve is the preferred technique. Many scud patterns are tied on a deeply bent hook, because a resting or dead scud stays in the fetal position, while the swimming scud is almost straight.

Sowbugs — Aquatic sowbugs are similar to scuds in water preferences and often co-exist in the same areas, especially in areas of heavy aquatic plant growth. Sowbugs are heavily segmented and are quite similar in appearance to scuds, the major difference being that whereas the scud's legs protrude from the underside of the insect, the sowbug's legs protrude from its sides. Sowbugs should be fished in much the same way as scuds, in mostly gray or gray/olive imitations.

Crayfish — Crayfish are the largest of the freshwater crustaceans. They look like a baby lobster and can grow up to 6 inches long. The smaller crayfish (crawdads), which are very important to larger trout where they exist in numbers, are 1/2 to 1 1/2 inches long. Crayfish are generally brownish in color with some color variations of red, orange, blue, olive and gray.

Shortly after shedding their exoskeleton, crawfish have a soft shell and a slight pinkish/light brown coloration. This is the life-form stage that trout most like to feed on. Even though they are considerably larger than the other foods we have been talking about in this book, the smaller crayfish fall squarely in the size range that is most preferred by trout.

Many elaborate imitations have been concocted to better imitate crayfish, but a Brown Woolly Bugger has taken many more trout than any other imitation.

A crayfish flees backwards with rapid kicks of its tail, so most imitations are tied with the claws trailing behind. Although crayfish are routinely imitated by most bass anglers, trout anglers rarely use crayfish patterns, even though they can be a major trout food. That is changing as ideas about fly fishing and total imitation change.

Daphnia — Daphnia, called "water fleas," and other very small, shrimp-like crustaceans are generally important only to very small fish, but in some lakes they are also a popular diet for large trout and kokanee salmon. Lake fish swim through clouds of these micro-sized crustaceans with their mouths open, feeding voraciously. Fly patterns to imitate individual daphnia are obviously impractical, but larger patterns that imitate a cluster of these edibles are often very effective in large lakes. Scud, Wooly

Worm, Barber Pole, Canadian Brown Leech, and San Juan Worm patterns are often taken for daphnia clusters or other small crustaceans.

TERRESTRIALS

Terrestrials refer to land-based insects that fall, jump, fly, get washed into, or get blown onto, the waters where trout live. Ants, beetles and grasshoppers are the most well known, but there are hundreds of species such as crickets, moths, leaf hoppers, jassids, maggots, inchworms and cicadas, that are important at certain times and places. Trout will very often develop a taste for these terrestrials as if they were manna from heaven. Even during big hatches of aquatic insects, trout will very often give preference to certain terrestrials.

Ants — Ants have a tangy acid taste that trout just seem to love. Ants are generally deposited on the water by falling off streamside vegetation or by being washed off the bank when water levels rise. There are also some large flights of flying ants in some localities, and when they are abundant, you can be sure the trout notice it. If you see a trout feeding along a bank and your hatch-imitating flies are not working, try an ant pattern and get a good drift over the trout. Then watch out.

Beetles — Along the same lines, beetles are a preferred food of many trout, when available. Ants and beetles are often called "hatch busters," because trout that are apparently feeding selectively on a certain stage of a hatch will automatically take these terrestrials when they pass.

Ants and beetles are difficult to fish unless you use a two-fly indicator rig (which is discussed in detail on pp. 96-100), one of which would be a highly visible dry fly.

Grasshoppers — Grasshoppers are commonly eaten by trout and are a favorite way for some anglers to fish. Particularly on windy days in meadow streams, trout go nuts on these large edibles. Small hoppers, those tied on #16 to #10 hooks, are rarely used by anglers that prefer using larger flies. The result is that in well-fished areas trout will key in on the smaller-sized hoppers, which are also more plentiful.

An important characteristic of grasshoppers is their trailing legs. Remember that trout often key in on one aspect of their foods and exclude all else. Legs are often the triggering key to grasshopper imitations. Rubber legs or trimmed and bent hackle stems used as legs will make any hopper pattern better. As an experiment, I tried a hopper pattern that consisted of nothing but rubber legs tied to a bare hook, and still took a number of hopper-feeding trout. This should tell you that even small hopper patterns should have appropriately sized and shaped legs.

There are so many small terrestrial insects that a whole book could be dedicated to that subject. If you want to know what terrestrials to use on a given day, just search the stream bank closely. Look at streamside vegetation and if you see a preponderance of any one terrestrial, you may be sure the trout are aware of them also.

TROUT JUNK FOOD

Trout junk food is, of course, not really junk food, but a variety of natural edibles that were once considered unworthy of imitation by any gentleman who angled for trout or salmon. Now, the modern definition of fly fishing has broadened to include all species of fish and imitations of all their foods. Trout have traditionally been viewed as insectivorous, but they are meat eaters too. In fact, trout will eat just about anything around that they can get into their mouths. Nothing that appears edible goes untouched. I've watched trout eat cigarette butts, clumps of moss, chicken bones, corn chips and Wonder Bread.

Their natural junk foods include fish eggs, dead salmon flesh, aquatic worms, minnows, and snails. Periodically they will also feed on critters like leeches, salamanders, frogs, mice, baby birds, and each other.

Eggs — Because they are so full of nutrition and are often abundant during spawning seasons, trout and salmon eggs are the most important of the junk foods. Trout often eat eggs to the exclusion of all other foods. The salmon runs in Alaska are world famous for attracting large rainbow trout. Alaskan rainbows would be small or non-existent without salmon eggs. A trout in the Lake Iliamna region of Alaska may increase its body weight 25 to 50 percent during the two or three months when salmon are in the river on the spawn!

Even where no salmon are present, almost all trout feed on eggs sometime during the year. Browns, brook, char and lake trout spawn in the fall. Rainbow, cutthroat and golden trout spawn in the spring or early summer. The eggs dropped by mature female trout and the eggs that escape the spawning beds are sometimes crushed by other spawning fish, or are eaten by pre-spawn, post-spawn, and spawning groupie trout.

Most eggs are small, only 5 to 6 mm in diameter, and each species has a particular color that ranges from pink and red for salmon eggs to orange and peach for trout eggs. Eggs bleached by the water get a pink, peach or light amber coloration. If possible, get a sample of the natural eggs and match the size and color to your imitations. Color and size matching are important on eggs, as in many areas where trout feeding on eggs are fished heavily, these fish naturally become more selective than trout that see little fishing pressure. Hook size is seldom critical, but it is a good idea to match the hook size with the trout size.

Remember, when I say "small egg patterns" I am referring to natural-sized egg patterns. Most people mistakenly use egg imitations that are two to five times larger than the naturals.

Salmon Flesh — In Alaska, once salmon spawn and die they begin to decompose and break apart in the streams, and the chunks of flesh are eaten by trout that are stocking up for the approaching winter. At that time, when dead salmon carcasses start decomposing and breaking apart, and cold weather is approaching, trout will begin feeding voraciously on dead salmon flesh, as if the fish sense the coming lean times of winter. To some, the thought of trout gorging themselves on dead salmon parts can sound grotesque, but it's a natural food that I like to think of as "salmon jerky" for trout.

In large streams with swift currents, the salmon flesh chunks, which are usually cream to ginger-colored, may be quite large, and are usually imitated with a big streamer pattern, usually a Ginger Bunny Bug or a Zonker. In many streams, however, the chunks that the trout prefer are much smaller. A small Zonker (1/2 to 1 inch long) does a much better job and is nicer to fish, too. It is best presented with a natural drift, much as a nymph would be, or swung very slowly.

Worms — Aquatic worms are present in many streams and trout feed on them quite voraciously when they are plentiful. Some look like a night crawler and others look more like a small red worm. The smaller versions of San Juan Worms will imitate the aquatic red worms and also bloodworms, which are actually blood-red midge larvae.

Mini-Minnows — Most streamer patterns that imitate mini-minnows are conventionally tied on #6 to #2 hooks. But many minnows that trout feed on are considerably smaller than that. Sucker minnows, dace, sculpins, shiners, salmon fry, trout fry, etc., often end up as a trout's dinner; yet few anglers use the smaller versions of streamers, doggedly following the old "big fly, big fish" theory. But streamers of from 1/2 to 1 1/2 inches long (and sometimes smaller) are often deadly for big trout in clear water. Trout feeding on minnows are prone to early morning and evening fish feeds. Oversized trout cruise the shallows of lakes and rivers looking for hapless minnows. Streamers are most effective when the fish are in a chasing mood. But all is not necessarily lost if they are not. In heavily fished waters, the trout become selective and good imitations of specific baitfish or good suggestive patterns can provide all the action you can handle, if the right factors are there.

Sometimes trout prefer streamers fished almost like nymphs, deep and on a natural drift. Trout that are feeding on migrating salmon fry can get keyed in on one type of fish and other flies will not be accepted. This is the feeding behavior of a trout that has more than enough to eat and can afford to be picky. When fished like a nymph (but with a little tension on the line), small streamers that accurately imitate salmon fry can be deadly.

Snails — Aquatic snails are fed upon by trout regularly. Actually, some trout feed so heavily that their stomachs are crunchy with the shells of snails. Snails are usually colored a drab brown, olive or tan. They can be fished with a dead-drift or slow-sinking presentation, followed by a twitch/rest retrieve.

OVERLEAF: *Palomino caddis.*

CHAPTER THREE

SELECTING SMALL FLY PATTERNS

THE FLY SELECTION PROCESS

When deciding which small fly to tie on your line first, observation, experimentation, imitation and past experience should all determine your choice. Nothing is a substitute for having experience and confidence with a pattern. But to gain that confidence, you need to experiment and learn how to fish various flies. You cannot get confidence in streamers if you only put one on after everything you've tried has failed. You cannot improve your nymphing technique if you seldom nymph. You must combine the information you read and hear with your own practical experience and experimentation. Just decide that you are going to learn more about small flies and then routinely plan for your fishing trip to include a good deal of experimentation. This gives your trip direction and will keep it quite interesting and educational, even on a slow fishing day.

So much is said about "secret" or "deadly" fly patterns that many anglers automatically think that if they are not catching trout it is because they do not have the right fly. In reality, the right fly is only a start. Presentation with the right fly in the right place at the right time to the right fish all comes together for fishing success. When reading about the fly patterns in this chapter, keep in mind that they are not a magic potion, but simply one ingredient in an intelligently planned system of fly fishing.

I will be mentioning some of my favorite small fly patterns. But this book is no Bible, so even though I hope what I have to say about the patterns I have developed confidence in will be of interest and assistance to you, you need to develop your own.

There are four things to consider when choosing a fly. (None of these things would necessarily be the flies that I recommend, or what your buddy uses, or what the fly shop recommends, or what some magazine article told you to use, or even what flies you now have in your box.) *You need to ask yourself what the fish wants today, in this particular water, at this specific time.* After all, you are the one on the water, observing what is happening, making the decisions, and doing the fishing.

First, consider the depth you need to fish. Are fish rising everywhere or are they more likely to be nymphing or feeding on scuds, eggs, etc.? If fish are feeding near the surface, are they feeding on insect emergers, emerged adults, egg-laying adults, spent adults or terrestrials?

Second is size and shape of the fly. What is the appropriate size and shape? Are the trout being selective today? Have they been fished over a good deal? Will medium-sized flies likely be rejected? And what is the size of the naturals on the water?

Third is the style of fly. Would covering the water with attractors be a good place to start? Are the trout going to be selective on a particular hatch? Is exact imitation called for? Would hatch busters, such as terrestrials, streamers, eggs, or aquatic worms, be productive? What shape of fly would catch the trout's attention best?

Fourth is color. It is not the most important consideration, but it can make a difference. Should you follow the old maxim, "Dark day, dark fly. Bright day, bright fly?" Is this a day when color will be important in fly selection? Should your flies' color be what is considered to be an attractor color (for example, the red and white of a Royal Wulff), a suggestive color (for example, the natural dull colors of a Hare's Ear), or a match-the-hatch color (for example, an exact imitation of a Blue-Winged Olive)?

Proper fly selection can often be simply a matter of asking yourself the right questions.

ATTRACTOR FLIES FOR FUN

If you have not yet read the preceding section in the book on trout feeding behavior, do so or you may not understand some of what will be discussed here.

Attractor flies are flies that have built in "triggers." They may trigger curiosity, aggression, parallel memories, imprinting or just plain old hunger. Some actually imitate certain foods or will trigger a feeding response because one aspect of the attractor fly is what triggers feeding. Many attractor dry flies have white wings, as white seems to be one of the best triggers for trout. Many also have peacock herl or hackle colors, rubber legs, or some sort of flash material that attracts hits.

The **Royal Wulff** has long been a favorite attractor. Because of its white wings, the Royal Wulff is not only easy for the angler to see, it also exhibits many of the triggers that attractor flies are famous for. This pattern works well from early summer through fall. Use large sizes in the evenings during mid-summer, and small sizes the rest of the time. Try #20 to #16 Royal Wulffs during

Small Attractor and Suggestive Imitations

hatches as a hatch buster. Wulffs work well during caddis hatches and can also imitate flying ants and mayflies.

The **Humpy**, alias **Goofus Bug**, is one of the best all-around dry flies because it is suggestive of many things but imitates nothing exactly. It can be perceived as an adult caddis, egg-laying caddis, emerging caddis, spent-wing caddis, emerging mayfly, adult mayfly, spent mayfly, stonefly adult, beetle, flying ant, midge cluster, grasshopper, stillborn or crippled insect, or just trigger a feeding response through parallel imprinting. It floats well in fast water — which is where it works best — and is relatively easy to see. In small sizes it can imitate various hatches, but is just different enough to catch the fish's eye.

The **Adams** dry fly has been around for years. This time-tested pattern can imitate many species of mayflies, midges and craneflies. It even works well during caddis hatches. It would be hard to improve upon this pattern, but the **Adams Parachute** (tied parachute-style, with the hackle wound around a single white wing) is deadly during small mayfly or midge hatches. It floats better, is easy to see, and works well in many hatch situations. As trout get selective, go to smaller sizes (#22 to #16).

The **Gray Halladay**, designed by Bart Halladay, is an excellent attractor or suggestive pattern for fishing small hatches such as mayflies, midges and craneflies. Its combination of peacock thorax, grizzly hackle and segmented body attracts trout for several reasons.

Trude-style **flies** have a downwing of elk hair or calf's tail. They are great flies for appealing to parallel imprinted trout. Fish them anytime during the summer or fall, but especially during and after the stonefly and caddis hatches. **California Trudes**, **Lime Trudes**, **Black Trudes** and **Royal Trudes** are popular anywhere where trout seem to like attractor flies. The smaller you get in fly size, the more selective the trout you can fool.

Prince Nymphs and **Zug Bugs** are two of the best attractor nymphs for searching water. If you are not really familiar with a stretch of stream, tie one or two attractor nymphs on and work a variety of water until you find where the trout are concentrated. Most people use these nymph patterns in larger sizes, but #20 to #14 versions work better for selective trout. During non-hatch periods these are great "Snicker's Bar" kinds of flies for getting trout to feed between meals.

The **Hare's Ear** is one of the all-time best producers for nymphers because of its high rating on the varied perception factor index. It can imitate a mayfly nymph, mayfly emerger (greased up), cased-caddis larva, caddis pupa, small stonefly nymph, scud, sowbug, snail, cranefly larva, midge larva or a variety of other aquatic critters. For selective trout, best sizes are from #24 to #16.

The **Pheasant Tail Nymph** accounts for more selective trout than any other nymph because of its clean nymphal shape, its ability to imitate various mayfly and stonefly nymphs, and because its peacock herl thorax attracts trout. One variation, the **Flashback Nymph**, is excellent in any size for trout anywhere. Its extra flash seems to catch the trout's attention. When trout are hyper-selective, stick with flies #16 or smaller. To imitate a midge with this pattern, just cut the tail and legs off.

The **Squirrel Nymph** is a good search pattern that can imitate various nymphs and larvae. It's another nymph that is most frequently tied large, but tied in small sizes it becomes more effective for selective trout that are feeding on midges, mayflies, scuds or stoneflies.

MAYFLY IMITATIONS

When a mayfly hatch has been identified, get a feel for the natural's size, shape and color to imitate it accurately. Matching the hatch is an interesting way to approach selective feeders, but remember to keep an open mind for other types of patterns such as attractors, terrestrials, and nymphs, even when some fish are rising to mayfly adults. To accurately imitate the various life-form stages of mayflies, you need patterns of the nymph, floating nymph, emerging adult, emerged adult with upright wings and trailing shuck, the mayfly dun, the egg-laying spinner and the spent-wing spinner. Cripples and stillborn duns can also be important at times.

Don't worry, it's not as complicated as all that. Nymphs can be greased to imitate floating nymphs. Duns can be clipped down so they sit lower in the water to imitate emergers, and so on. If trout are rejecting nymph and dun

Small Mayfly Imitations

patterns, they are likely feeding on the transition or emerger stages of the mayfly, right in the surface film.

Thorax Duns are great hatch-matching dry flies that can be fished to imitate the duns or clipped down to imitate the emerger. They come in various colors and sizes to imitate almost any mayfly hatch. The hackle is generally clipped V-shaped on the bottom and with the tail tied splayed to allow the pattern to sit evenly on the surface.

No-Hackle dry flies are good hatch-matchers for picky feeders on slow, flat water. But they do not float or perform well in fast water. In fast water, switch to a Thorax Dun, an Adams Parachute or a Humpy, depending on the roughness and velocity of the water. No-hackles are more durable than they look, and will work even when the wings are shredded. Foam-wing versions float best.

Parachute-style flies come in many body colors to match natural mayflies. Some have wings that are the natural color and others have white calf's tail or Z-Lon wings which are easier to see and add an attractor dimension to these imitative patterns. Because parachute flies float so well, they can be fished in any type of water. They make great strike indicators for small nymphs trailed behind. One variation that I find quite effective is a trailing shuck instead of a tail. Just substitute brown Z-Lon or soft brown partridge feathers for the regular tail, and put fly floatant only on the wing and hackle so that the tail sinks. Parachute patterns with white wings are an especially good way to be able to see dry flies, even in the most effective sizes, #22 to #16.

Floating Nymphs, which imitate the mayfly that is just starting to emerge from its nymphal shuck, have a ball of dubbing or closed-cell foam that supports the fly in the surface film. While they are difficult to see when fished as a single fly, they are so effective at times that no one who fishes mayfly hatches should be without some. They are also easily fished with a two-fly indicator rig, with the nymph placed as a dropper behind a visible dry fly such as an Adams Parachute or a Royal Wulff.

CDC Emergers come in a wide assortment now and are quite effective imitations of the emerging duns. They imitate the duns that are not yet completely emerged from their nymphal shucks, a favorite stage for trout to feed on because the insect is so vulnerable at this stage. CDCs are reasonable imitations of cripples and stillborn duns, as well. Floating nymph and CDC patterns are more effective than dry flies in many hatch situations. But they must be presented accurately and naturally to be effective.

Biot Nymphs are accurate imitations of small mayfly nymphs — including the smallest nymphs — for the most selective trout. In clear water they can be fished as small as #24, but sizes from #20 to #16 are easier to fish. This small pattern is incredibly effective in nymphing shallow water for selective fish. In shallow water, selective trout feed voraciously on small nymphs, but few fly fishermen fish them properly. In shallow water or in the tails of pools, grease up the leader to within several inches of the fly and watch the leader track as a strike indicator. In water where trout are feeding more than a foot deep, use a small strike indicator and micro split-shot to fish the appropriate depth.

The **Harrop Blue Wing** is an accurate mayfly nymph pattern that can also be used as an emerger just under the surface. Used in #22 to #16 sizes, it is a deadly pattern on finicky trout that are holding just under the surface.

Pheasant Tail Nymphs, which can also be fished as attractors, have long been among some of the best mayfly nymph imitations. Variations include using dyed or bleached pheasant tail. The bleached version imitates the light-colored mayfly and stonefly nymphs quite well. Dyed black, purple, olive/green or orange, a Pheasant Tail can often trigger selective trout when the regular colors are not working. Keep in mind that trout can actually get used to certain patterns that are presented to them a lot, and changes in color, flash, or size of the pattern often turn the key.

The **Quigley's Cripple** in small sizes imitates the crippled emerging duns that just keep floating around until a trout eats them.

Spent-Wing Mayfly patterns (usually referred to as **spinners**) can save your morning and evening fishing when trout are rising to a seemingly invisible hatch. Look closely in the scum lines in back eddies to see if these spent insects are being collected there. Imitations of this insect are difficult to see unless you use white Z-Lon or Crystal Flash in the wings to reflect light better. The wings of the naturals seem to sparkle anyway, so a flashy wing does not usually detract from the fly's effectiveness. All mayfly species have a spent stage, but certain small may-flies, such as Blue-Winged Olives and Tricos, have large spinner falls that the trout definitely prefer. Long, light tippets are usually necessary with these type patterns, as are accurate and delicate presentations.

MIDGE IMITATIONS

Midges, the most prolific and one of the smallest aquatic insects in many streams, lakes, sloughs, and ponds, are never ignored as a food source by trout. Midge imitations include larva, which look like mosquito larva, the pupa, the suspended pupa, the emerging midge adult, the midge cluster, the egg-laying midge and spent midge.

The **Griffith's Gnat** is the all time best adult midge pattern. It can imitate the emerging midge, a small midge cluster, an egg-laying midge or a spent midge. By trim-ming the hackle short, it also becomes a good suggestive nymph or pupa pattern. If small mayflies are emerging, trout will also take a Griffith's Gnat, mistaking it for a mayfly emerger or dun. It should be fished on #24 to #14 hooks. If egg-laying midges are present, it can be skit-tered, but is most useful fished with a natural drift. With a two-fly indicator rig, place an emerger, pupa or larva pattern behind it as a trailer and it becomes one of the most effective ways to fish midge hatches. Variations include dubbed bodies instead of peacock herl, trailing shucks as a tail, or a white wing for better visibility. As a match-hatcher, suggestive fly, or even attractor fly, the Griffith's Gnat's versatility makes it a must for every fly rodder's fly box.

Brown, Black, Olive and **White Midges** are the hatch-matchers. They are used mainly when you know that the

Small Midge Imitations

trout are feeding on individual, adult midges. Accurate and delicate presentations are a must. They can be clipped down to imitate emergers.

The **Serendipity** is a popular midge pupa imitation. Its body consists of twisted Z-Lon or Larva Lace and a clipped deer-hair head. When using this pattern on flat water, grease your leader with fly floatant up to within several inches of the fly. Use the leader track or another fly as a strike indicator. It can be fished right in the surface film or even down near the bottom, in sizes #24 to #16.

The **Larson Sparkle Midge** is a good pattern for fishing small flies in water that is a little off-color. The Antron fibers at the head of the pattern collect light and are easily seen by the trout.

The **Larva Lace Midge** is a simple but effective midge larva pattern. Larva Lace is slipped over the hook's eye, and then thread is wound over the tubing to create a segmented body. A head of peacock herl, ostrich herl, or dubbing can be added, as well as a wingcase of Z-Lon, to imitate the pupa. It can be tied down to as small as a #22 in yellow, brown, black, olive, red and tan. An infinite number of variations is possible by changing the Larva Lace's tubing and thread colors.

The **Brassie** has been a standby midge larva pattern for many years. The body is copper wire and the head is ostrich or peacock herl. It should be fished in sizes from #14 to #24. It is naturally weighted and best fished deep in riffles and runs.

The **Suspender Midge** is similar to a Floating Nymph in that it is constructed with a ball of dubbing or closed-cell foam to suspend the fly right at the surface. It is fished in the vertical position. To improve visibility, it can be double-rigged behind a dry fly.

CADDIS IMITATIONS

Caddis patterns have long been quite general in nature because the naturals vary only slightly in size and color. Some modern patterns go the extra distance to imitate the pupal and emerger stages which the trout often feed on more than the adult or larval stages. The larva imitations imitate either the free-roaming, grub-like larva or the cased-caddis variety. Pupa imitations are usually tied loose and with sparkle materials to mimic the translucent pupal stage. Pupa emergers and adults with trailing shucks work well. The newly emerged adults depart the stream so quickly that they are not very important, but the cripples, egg-laying, and spent-caddis life-forms have imitations that work well.

The **Elk-Hair Caddis** is a good imitation of caddis adults for fast water. Since elk hair is often very difficult to work with in smaller sizes, coastal deer wings in regular or bleached colors will work best. I usually like to carry one light pattern and one dark pattern. The body color of

Small Caddis Imitations

this imitation is not as important as it is with mayflies. Small caddis patterns also imitate small stonefly adults.

Partridge Caddis are better patterns for selective feeders in flat water and also better imitate the micro-caddis hatches that are often very dark. These small, dark patterns are very difficult to see, so you may want to fish them behind a larger dry fly. Partridge Caddis can be used in any sizes from #10 to #22, but they don't float as well as the Elk-Hair Caddis.

The **LaFontaine Sparkle Emergent Caddis** and **Deep Sparkle Caddis Pupa** are a great pair of flies to imitate the pupal stages of the caddis. The Deep Sparkle is tied weighted and fished suspended a few inches under the surface or along the bottom, as with any nymph. It is effective in lakes and streams alike. It is usually fished on the swing or with an active retrieve, but it will work being drifted naturally too. Letting the fly sink and then raising the rod as it passes in front of some caddis-feeding trout can be a very effective technique with this pattern. The Emergent Caddis has a lock of deer hair tied on top to imitate the adult's wing beginning to emerge. It should be fished right up in the surface film, either with a natural drift or on the swing. Because it sits low in the water and is difficult to see, it is often fished behind an Elk-Hair Caddis or some other strike indicator pattern.

Nemes-style Soft Hackle patterns are traditional caddis wet flies with green, orange, yellow or tan bodies. They can simulate mayfly nymphs or diving caddis as well. Their soft, barred partridge hackles give the impression of life and natural swimming movement. Such soft-hackle flies have been around for years, but they are making a comeback in popularity now that they have been recognized as imitations of specific insects. The pattern is most often fished on #12 and #14 hooks, but smaller sizes will sometimes clean up on selective trout. If the soft hackle is too thick, trim some of it off.

The **Palomino Caddis** patterns, developed by Brett Smith, are a new series of flies that are beginning to gain a following. The pattern's extended body with micro-chenille gives a natural-bodied silhouette to the fly. It comes in dry-fly, pupa and cased-caddis versions. The fly is best tied on short-shank, wide-gaped hooks.

The **Chamois Caddis Nymph** is very effective when trout are feeding on free-roaming caddis or other grub-like larvae. Chamois Caddis, #16 to #20, take selective feeders and also work well as an attractor nymph. In small sizes it is one of the best patterns for trout that are feeding in a small strike zone. You can change its colors easily with a waterproof felt marker. A soft-hackled pattern makes a good pupal imitation.

Peeking Caddis imitate the cased caddis that has a bit of its body showing out of the case. Since caddis are so widespread, such caddis larva patterns are effective almost anywhere trout exist. Every angler should have a few caddis larva patterns in his fly box. The pattern is often tied weighted, and works well in lakes as well as streams.

STONEFLY IMITATIONS

Stoneflies are not usually associated with small fly techniques, but there are a number of small stonefly species that are quite important at certain times and on certain waters. The stonefly has no emerger stage to imitate. This is because the insect crawls to shore-side vegetation before emerging. The nymphs of some stoneflies have a life span of several years so that in the waters where they exist, trout are very accustomed to seeing stonefly nymphs

Small Stonefly Imitations

year-round. Small stonefly nymphs can be imitated with either Hare's Ear or Pheasant Tail nymphs.

The **Tullis Rubber-Leg Stonefly** is an effective pattern fished deep. In small sizes, the pattern imitates the immature stage of larger varieties, as well as the nearly mature nymphs of the small stoneflies.

Little Yellow Stones, often called **Yellow Sallies**, are common on many streams, but are seldom imitated. Some of the adult stoneflies are bright yellow and others are a chartreuse green. Tied on #18 to #14 hooks, they are especially effective for the trout that get keyed in on these particular insects.

Burk's CDC Stones make good stonefly patterns. They have a CDC wing tied Trude-style with an extended ultra-chenille body. Fished on #18 to #14 hooks, they imitate stoneflies and some caddis.

Small Black and **Dark Brown Stoneflies** are imitations of naturals that will often hatch at the same time as the Yellow Sallies. There is also a variety that hatches in wintertime.

Small Brown Stonefly patterns imitate adult naturals that can sometimes overshadow caddis hatches in early summer. But because they are low profile insects, they are often overlooked by fly fishermen. But if you are not able to find them present on the river, you can be sure the trout know they are there.

CRUSTACEAN IMITATIONS

Scuds are effectively imitated with **Plastic-Back Scuds** and small **Fur Nymphs**. In spring, the larger versions work well, but later in the year, #22 to #16 patterns work best. In streams they should be drifted naturally like a nymph. In lakes they should be wind-drifted, or retrieved with short, fast strips.

Crayfish patterns abound, but few fly fishermen actually have the faith to fish them. Crayfish are not always available to trout, but where they exist in any substantial numbers, you can bet that the bigger trout know they are there. They are an enormous meal. And be sure to remember that even the most selective trout who are ignoring medium-sized flies and showing a preference for small flies can be opportunistic on very large food sources when they are available.

Crayfish can be tied on #12 to #2/0 hooks. The smaller patterns are perfect mouth-sized food for trout. The best pattern I've used is a **Brown Woolly Bugger,** because, I believe, the trout will take it for a leech, crayfish, minnow, nymph or tadpole. It is one of the all-time best suggestive patterns ever designed. And this great pattern has caught trout for me all over the world. But again, few fly fishermen use small versions. Other good crayfish imitations are the **Borger Crayfish**, **Whitlock Crayfish**, **Clouser Crayfish**, or **Tullis Wiggle Crayfish**.

Sowbug patterns are few, but any buggy gray or olive nymph, or any scud pattern, can be taken for a sowbug. A **Fur Nymph** or a **Plastic-Back Sowbug** will do the job if fished right along the bottom.

Daphnia might sound like something crazy to fish with, because you would need to tie them on tiny, #64 hooks! But they are, in fact, subject to imitation, because they often clump up or cluster in schools in lakes. A very small, red, thin-bodied **Woolly Bugger**, **Canadian Brown Leech** or **Byron's Killer** can attract daphnia-feeding trout; and since trout will also take these flies for damselfly or dragonfly nymphs, they are effective lake patterns anytime. Use #14 to #6 patterns.

TERRESTRIAL IMITATIONS

When it comes to late summer and early fall fishing, terrestrials are the focus of many anglers that are in the know. As trout get hyper-selective on the prevalent hatches, they also get more and more interested in terrestrials. Terrestrials are the ultimate hatch busters.

Grasshoppers can provide some of the most exciting trout fishing action of the summer. The large boils on hopper patterns cast right along shore can be extremely exciting. Small grasshoppers are more plentiful than their larger cousins, and when trout begin to feel the pressure of larger grasshopper patterns being fished over them, they become very size-conscious, and prefer instead the smaller, less often imitated hoppers. Few people fish #10 or smaller hoppers, but they can work extremely well. No matter the size, make sure you use hoppers that have legs.

Ants can be made from a variety of materials — closed-cell foam, dubbing, floss, or even cork. The floss-body version is fished underwater; the others are fished in the surface film. Where ants are available to the trout, the ant is a pattern you must have if you plan on fooling selective feeders on small flies. Ants come in sizes from #24 to #14, in black, cinnamon and red. Because they are practically impossible to see in small sizes, they are best fished behind a small attractor fly or parachute dun. The trout will come to investigate the larger fly and incidentally see the ant. It's a great combo that is both easy to fish and deadly. Legs are important but don't get carried away — ants have six legs, not 120. If you are lucky enough to be fishing when a big flight of flying ants is blown onto the water, quickly tie on a flying ant pattern with a Royal Trude attractor, and hold on, because the trout are getting ready to go crazy!

Small Terrestrial Imitations

Beetles are fished in the same way and the same places as ants. Concentrate along the shoreline, current edges, and back eddies. Foam and dyed black deer hair are the most popular body material versions, tied on #20 to #10 hooks. The underbody is fashioned from dubbing, peacock herl or pearlescent Mylar. A bright spot of T-shirt paint on its back makes the pattern much more visible. Legs made of bent deer hair or rubber make the pattern more effective. Use beetles for selective feeders that are not responding well to your hatch-matching flies.

Crickets in small sizes with white or black wings are deadly on the hot dog-days of summer. Fish them to rising fish or just cast blind, especially along grassy banks. As with hoppers, trailing legs are an important feature to trigger hits.

Many other terrestrial insects, such as **jassids** and **leaf hoppers** are important at times. Most can be imitated with a small Trude-style pattern in black or peacock herl body with a white or black wing and black or brown hackle. A bright green leaf hopper can be imitated with a bright green wing on a Griffith's Gnat. **Green inchworms**, which drop into the stream from shoreline vegetation, can be imitated with dyed green deer hair lashed to the hook with a spiral wrap to cause segmentations.

The **Spider** pattern is tied on a small hook and dressed with an extremely long hackle and tails. It may be taken by trout as a spider natural, but usually the fish mistake it for an egg-laying cranefly. Proper technique for this pattern is to skitter it on the surface of the water with the rod held high. The rises are usually dramatic — which is the most fun about fishing this pattern — but fish are really not hooked too often. Popular sizes are #18 to #14.

TROUT JUNK FOOD IMITATIONS

San Juan Worms are treated disdainfully as a joke by some anglers, but the fact is that they are superb imitations of two natural trout foods, aquatic red worms and blood midges. You are ignoring a significant element of the art of fly fishing if you refuse to use patterns like these.

The San Juan Worm pattern that is intended to imitate the aquatic red worm is usually tied with red ultrachenille. The natural red worm is actually more of a rusty brown color, but the bright red San Juan Worm is also an imitation of the blood midge, a bright red midge that can elongate itself like a leech.

A better pattern, the **Chamois Worm**, can be created by cutting chamois cloth into thin strips and coloring them red or rust with a waterproof art marker. When wet, the chamois is much softer and more pliable than ultrachenille. A Chamois Worm tied on a small weighted hook is very lifelike.

Small Trout Junk Food Imitations

Most people tie San Juan Worms and Chamois Worms on a large English bait hook which, in my opinion, looks too large and stiff. Use smaller hooks and sizes to imitate more lifelike versions of these patterns, and on selective trout you may be surprised at the comparative results.

Glo-Bugs have been around for nearly two decades. Salmon and steelhead flies that imitate egg clusters have been around even longer. When egg fly patterns first started making the rounds, most fly fishers just scoffed at them. The first time a fishing buddy showed me one and asked for my opinion, I laughed and said, "Fake salmon eggs will never work." He just smiled and proceeded to catch seven trout in seven casts! Boy, I got my attitude adjusted, and have fished egg patterns ever since at those times when trout are obviously keyed in on eggs.

With the general acceptance of egg patterns in the fly rodder's arsenal has come a larger variety to choose from. The standard has been the Glo-Bug, but soon after came the **Iliamna Pinkies**, **Nuclear Roe Bugs**, **Meg-A-Eggs** and **Bead Eggs**. These later generations of the pattern represent not so much an improved design, but really just something different looking. They all work. But you have to be discriminating, just like the trout are. In heavily fished waters, trout can become keyed in on exact size and color, and will accept no substitute. The average Glo-Bug was once the size of a dime. Now egg patterns seldom exceed 7 mm, and 5 to 6 mm in diameter is even more natural. Hook size is not very important but body size and color is. Glo-Bugs should be fished with a natural drift, just like a nymph. Bead Eggs and small Nuclear Roe Bugs are best for selective trout on those waters where Glo-Bugs have been fished extensively.

Flesh Flies in small sizes are very effective for Alaskan trout in many streams in early fall. The most common pattern is a #2 **Ginger Bunny Bug**, but a #10 is more effective for trout in C & R waters. Fish this pattern with a natural drift or on a slow swing.

Leeches come in all sizes. You probably know that I'm going to tell you to use smaller size leeches, right? Right! Selective trout in clear water like smaller leeches much better than the monster patterns most anglers fish. If you can work a small **Marabou Leech** or **Woolly Bugger** slowly along the bottom, you'll get some large trout.

The **Borger Snail Fly** is used in lakes by stripping the line once or twice to get the trout's attention, then letting it sit for a few seconds and repeat. This triggers the trout's "think fast" reaction and it can often be very productive. In situations where you observe that trout are picking up snails on the surface, fish a floating version of the pattern.

However, generally speaking, most crustacean patterns should be fished close to the bottom or in channels between weedbeds.

MINI-MINNOW IMITATIONS

At one time there were streamer fishermen who made an art of their avocation, but it seems that fewer anglers fish streamers at high skill levels these days. Of course, a few still do, and they are the guys that catch large trout regularly. A good friend of mine who is a master streamer angler once caught and released a 17-pound brown trout from the Provo River, a well-fished stream near my hometown. And that fish was just one of 25 trout he caught on that same day! I think the main reason few fly fishermen fish streamers extensively today is that the large imitative streamers are hard to cast.

Of course, smaller versions are easier to cast, and are actually better suited to today's more selective trout. You can fish streamer patterns anytime. The trout are not always aggressive enough to chase streamers, but when they are, you can have excellent fishing.

Mini-Minnow Imitations

Many streams throughout the trout's range are inhabited by big trout that regularly feed on the fry of salmon, suckers, whitefish, and other small minnow-like species. For example, Alaska in June means fishing fry streamer imitations for the large native rainbows. The sockeye and other salmon fry that were spawned the previous summer are hatching, emerging from the gravel and beginning their migration down to the ocean. Trout stack up at lake outlets and eddies where the fry congregate and feed freely on the immature salmon. The trout just gobble them up, and an accurate imitation of the fry can often create great streamer fishing for larger trout.

Fry flies are small minnow imitations that are tied sparsely. Small bucktail patterns such as the **Black-Nosed Dace** and **Small Trout Bucktail Series** will work. Small saltwater flies such as a **Glass Minnow** or **Crazy Charlie** are also good, as are **Thunder Creek Special**, **Yolk Sac**, **Swim-Up Fry** and **Tullis Bead-Head Fry** streamer patterns. These should be tied on #14 to #8 hooks in natural colors. In late spring and early summer these small streamer patterns are particularly effective, but try them any time of year.

Sculpin patterns 1 to 2 inches long can trigger trout that are not feeding on hatches. These trout, who normally feed at low light or at night, can be the biggest trout in the watershed. Sculpin imitations should be fished deep with a short fast strip that makes the fly dart. They can be fished in any water type from rapids to high mountain lakes. Use sizes from #14 to #2, with smaller sizes for selective trout in clear water. Black, mottled brown, olive and gray/brown are the best colors with tan or crystal chenille bodies.

The **Wiggle Bug** is a fly pattern that I designed to imitate the swimming action of a number of various minnows, leeches, crayfish, tadpoles and nymphs. It is a hand-tied, lightweight, closed-cell foam fly that swims like a Flatfish lure. The fly performs superbly in murky water or at night, when the trout can feel the fly's swimming action through its lateral-line sensing system. Smaller versions of the Wiggle Bug, in sizes #10 to #2, are quite easy to cast, even on a 3-weight rod. This is a pattern I always carry with me. It can really turn trout on in certain waters.

Clouser Deep Minnows are becoming well known for their big fish catching abilities. Small sizes, tied like Crazy Charlies to imitate baitfish or fry, work very well because the lead eyes on the fly get the fly down where the bigger trout lie, and when tied sparsely can fool selective feeders in clear water.

All the fly patterns listed in this chapter are just a place to start. Once you realize what you are trying to imitate and have an idea on how and when the trout are feeding, you can come up with patterns that you prefer. Of course, there is no such thing as a magic fly that works everywhere, but using the criteria that I've given you so far, you should be able to intelligently choose small fly patterns for the waters you fish.

This next chapter deals with specific techniques for fishing small flies, which I consider far more important than what fly you use.

OVERLEAF: *Charlie Barnes fishing a streambed flat.*

CHAPTER FOUR

SMALL FLY PRESENTATION AND FISHING TECHNIQUES

There are a number of essential techniques involved in effectively presenting and fishing small flies to trout. Among them are casting, line mending and management, and after a successful presentation, hooking up and playing the fish. But a successful small fly presentation should actually begin not with the muscles of your casting arm when you first pick up your rod, but in the gray matter between your ears.

Before you make the first cast of the day, you should first study and think about the various factors over which you really have no control that will be influencing your presentation. Chief among them are the difficulty of seeing a small fly (and what steps you can take to counteract that problem); concentrating on the trout's strike zone; reading the water; understanding the principles of natural drift; and understanding the various drift levels at which trout feed in the water column. So let's examine these more or less "thoughtful" subjects first.

The wrong fly presented properly may catch fish, while the right fly presented improperly will result in a skunking. I believe that fly-fishing success is 75 percent presentation and 25 percent imitation, and some anglers whose opinion I respect think that the percentage is even higher than that. But no matter what fly you use, if you cannot see or otherwise track what is happening with your fly, there's really no sense in making a presentation at all. You might as well reel in your line and sit on the bank. This is a *visual* sport.

Being able to see small flies is tough, I admit, but that should not stop you even if you are legally blind. Here are several ways to track the fly and see trout takes even when you cannot actually see your fly.

The Two-Fly Indicator Rig

The two-fly indicator rig is an invaluable tool for small fly fishing, because the larger and more visible dry fly acts as a strike indicator for a smaller dry fly, or for an emerger, nymph or scud pattern rigged as a subsurface dropper. Also, if trout are feeding within 2 feet of the surface, or if they come up from deep in the water column to take a look at (and then reject) the larger attractor dry fly, the smaller dry or wet fly becomes a back-up pattern that trout will often take, almost without thinking.

Standard strike indicators will sometimes work well, of course. But trout frequently get accustomed to seeing strike indicators — particularly in shallow water — and learn to associate them with danger. I have actually seen fish stop feeding or move out of the way when a standard strike indicator went by. But the two-fly indicator rig solves that problem.

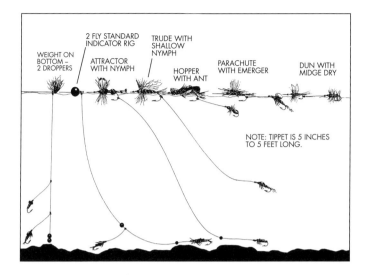

Two-Fly Indicator Rigs

The two-fly indicator rig is perhaps the best technique that has yet to be developed for small fly fishing. For the novice angler, it has its drawbacks, as sloppy casting and line management techniques, particularly in windy conditions, will frequently tangle the two flies and their monofilament together into a bird's nest — some of which are a wonder to behold.

But if you are a competent fly fisherman, there's simply no question in my mind, at least, that for small fly fishing — and for most nymphing as far as that goes — this is the way to fish. It simply makes the two flies more effective than each fished singly. It's sort of symbiotic. I've observed anglers fishing two flies properly improve their success rate from 30 to 150 percent!

A two-fly indicator rig basically consists of a visible floating dry fly tied in normal fashion to the end of the

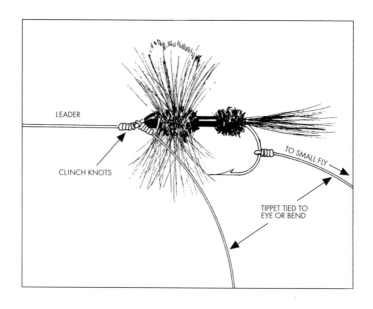

Method of Tying Clinch Knots in a Two-Fly Indicator Rig

leader, to which a length of tippet — say from 6 to 60 inches, depending upon the depth of the water — is tied to the hook eye or bend of the dry fly, and to which is then tied a smaller fly (the dropper). The three knots needed can all be tied with a standard improved clinch knot or a Trilene knot (but the Trilene will require going through the hook eye twice on the flies, which is an impossible task on very small flies). Micro-shot can be used with the rig if the larger pattern is buoyant enough to support the weight for a drift.

There are two principal reasons that this rig is such a great presentation instrument. First, of course, it allows the angler to see and track small flies. Not being able to see or track small flies is frustrating and the biggest reason most people don't fish them. Second, the two-fly indicator rig adds the capability for the angler to present two flies simultaneously to search at two different levels in the water column, or to test out two different patterns at the same water level.

The most popular combination for the rig is to use an attractor dry fly such as a Royal Wulff, a Humpy, or a Madame X as the indicator, and a small nymph such as a Pheasant Tail, Hare's Ear, Chamois Caddis, etc., as the dropper. I have tried out many combinations and have found that when no hatches are prevalent, an attractor fly combined with a small natural-looking nymph works best. If hatches are present, I'll go to two life-form stages of the same insect, such as a dun and a floating nymph.

Other effective doubles include an Elk-Hair Caddis with a LaFontaine Caddis Pupa; a White-Wing Parachute dry fly in a body color to match the natural dun with a mayfly emerger; a Griffith's Gnat with a midge pupa; a hopper with a scud; a cicada with a San Juan Worm; a Royal Wulff with an egg; a Thorax Dun with an ant; a Humpy with a beetle; an Adams with a Floating Nymph; a Henry's Fork Hopper with a Prince Nymph; a Double Ugly with a Serendipity; an Adams Parachute with a Flashback Pheasant Tail Nymph; and so on. The combinations become endless. A friend of mine has even used this type rig for Atlantic salmon, with a Bomber-type dry fly and a standard salmon wet fly as a dropper.

For nymphing the same philosophy can be followed quite successfully, tying two nymph patterns on your line, one as a terminal fly and one as a dropper, on a standard nymphing rig with a strike indicator. This rig can increase nymphing hook-ups as much as 100 percent.

In big lakes — where most anglers have an innate fear of using small flies — you should also experiment with using a small dropper fly behind your usual larger fly, and compare the results to single fly presentations. In fact, in almost any situation when you are fishing small flies, the two-fly rig will improve your catch rate.

Strike Indicators

Strike indicators (made from closed-cell foam, buoyant yarn, fly-line coating, cork or just a leader dressed with fly floatant) aid in strike detection with nymphs, of course; but they also work well with dry flies. Today, fly fishermen who don't occasionally use strike detectors are a vanishing breed as the benefits of strike indicators are becoming manifest to everyone. There are principally three: a strike indicator will help you detect hits much better; it will help you in determining if you are getting a natural drift; and it will assist you in preventing the fish from swallowing a fly too deeply, since the use of an indicator should increase your reaction time. Strike indicators are no longer just for beginners, but have become a valid tool for even the most experienced fly fishermen.

Indicators are just fun to watch, too. It gives you a more visual aspect to nymph fishing in lakes and streams. Regardless of your skill level, strike indicators will increase your success ratio. That makes them a valid tool and not some gimmick.

Indicators can be made from almost any buoyant material that is visible and not too bulky or air resistant so that it would impair the cast. Here are some favorite types and how to rig them.

Yarn Indicators — Yarn indicators can be made from natural wool, such as the material in Lefty's Strike Indicator, from synthetic tow yarn such as that used on Glo-Bug flies, or from frayed macrame yarn treated with fly floatant. Yarn indicators are easy to see, even in poor light conditions, but can be somewhat air resistant. They are

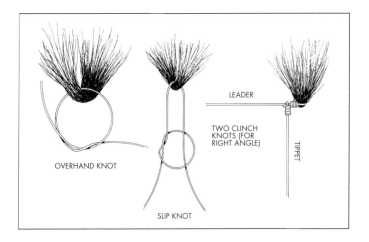

LEADER

TWO CLINCH
KNOTS (FOR
RIGHT ANGLE)

TIPPET

OVERHAND KNOT

SLIP KNOT

Yarn Indicator

attached to the leader by placing the material inside either
an overhand or slip knot that has been tied into the leader.
Another method that is gaining popularity is to tie the
yarn onto the end of the tapered leader and then clinch
knot the tippet material to the leader, so that there is a
90-degree angle between your leader and tippet during
the drift. This helps keep the fly directly under the indicator for a good natural drift and quick strike detection.

Hard Foam or Cork Indicators — Hard foam or cork
indicators come in many shapes and colors. Their size has
to be determined by the angler in relationship to the type
of fly he is using, and how large an indicator will be
required to maintain buoyancy. Brightly colored, larger
sizes are used for deep, fast water. Smaller, less brightly
colored sizes are great for shallow water nymphing with
micro-split shot. Small, brightly colored indicators can
even be used with small dry flies, to help track the drift
when you cannot see the fly well or when you do not want

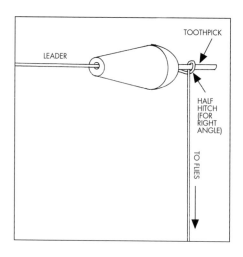

Foam or Cork Indicator

to use the two-fly indicator rig. A foam or cork indicator can be attached by threading it onto the leader and jamming a toothpick in the gap between the indicator's hole and the leader to secure it in place. For best results, place the toothpick in the gap on the side of the indicator that will be facing the fly, and then put a half-hitch knot around the toothpick. The half-hitch will keep the indicator from slipping during casting, and also will create a 90-degree angle to the leader to improve the drift and sink rate of the nymph. Some indicators now are sliced halfway through for easier attachment to and detachment from the leader. Some have rubber cores that allow you to twist the line inside the indicator to keep them from slipping.

Fly-line Coating Indicators — Fly-line coating indicators are pieces of floating fly-line coating that can be threaded up the leader and jammed over a knot for placement. They are poor indicators for weighted flies because they do not have much buoyancy, but are excellent for use

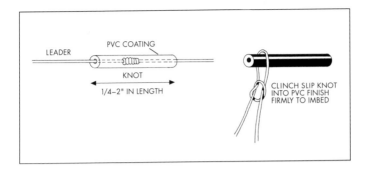

Fly-Line Coating Indicator

on shallow-water trout or for fishing unweighted emerger or dry-fly patterns. They are particularly useful when, because of current, weather, or light conditions, you desire to place multiple indicators along the leader and line for better visibility. Simply place the indicators at intervals up the leader and line, and if one sinks in fast water, the others can still be seen. Additionally, multiple indicators can help you read currents, strikes, and drift of the fly, by comparing the relative movement of the indicators.

Pinch or Roll-On Foam Indicators — Pinch or roll-on foam indicators are convenient but are generally not very adjustable and tend to come off while casting, contributing to the streamside trash problem.

Whatever strike indicator you prefer, it should generally be placed one to two times the depth of the water from the fly. For example, if the water is 3 feet deep, place the indicator 3 to 6 feet from the fly. Too long a distance between the fly and indicator and light hits will be difficult to detect. Too short a distance and your fly will not get down into the strike zone properly.

Whatever strike indicator you select, adjustability should be a paramount consideration, because the distance between the fly and the indicator will need to be changed with each type of fly and each depth of water in which you fish.

The size of the indicator you are using should change somewhat as you change the depth of water fished. If you are fishing a small indicator that does not support a weighted rig in deeper water, add another indicator, right next to it, for additional buoyancy.

Indicator color can be a factor on some waters. Of course, you want to be able to see the indicator, but you don't want the trout to be distracted by one. Orange, chartreuse and red are the easiest colors to see in fast, roiled water. But if you find a trout being distracted or spooked by such a brightly colored indicator, change to a pale yellow or white one. Some anglers use black yarn indicators in flat water with glare.

Reading strike indicator movement is more important than how you rig one. If you do not understand what the indicator is indicating, you will get less than ideal drifts and miss many strikes. Let's assume you've cast properly and are getting a good drift. The indicator should be drifting at about the same speed as the current (or slightly slower, if you are fishing along the bottom). Watch the indicator closely for any unusual movement or hesitation in its natural drift. If it sinks, hesitates or moves cross current, raise the rod immediately to set the hook or to dislodge your fly from a rock. But never assume that a hesitation is just the bottom.

Always assume that any aberration in natural drift — no matter how minor or slight — is a trout. If you will make this assumption, you will hook many more light-striking trout. When guiding, I always tell my clients to set the hook if it looks like a fish is breathing on the fly! It will amaze you how many times what you thought was the bottom or current turns out to be a trout. On such a movement, set the hook gently, but swiftly. Educated trout can spit out a fly extremely fast.

In areas where the trout are visible, keep your attention on the indicator, but let your peripheral vision work to search elsewhere in the water for flashes of a trout feeding or its mouth opening. Anything that increases your reaction time when nymphing is good. If your nymph is hitting the bottom too frequently, reduce the amount of weight being used.

The Lift/Drift Technique

Another method of whipping the visibility problem on small flies is the "lift/drift" technique. With this technique, even though your fly may be unsighted, estimate the point at which you think your fly is drifting into the trout's strike zone, and when it reaches that point, lift the rod to set the hook just as if you had actually seen the take. Sometimes this works. If not, simply lower your rod and allow your fly to drift a little while longer, and then lift the rod again.

Of course, this lift/drift method will not be effective unless you really get the timing just right, but it's better practice than fishing an unsighted small fly and merely hoping that somehow you will get lucky.

When you are presenting flies, such as caddis pupa imitations, that can be swung in the current, you can go more by feel than by sight. Trying to induce a take on the retrieve works on the same principle. Rather than relying on a visual stimulus to indicate when to set the hook, you should concentrate on your sense of touch. With this technique, your line should be tight and straight from your fingers to the fly so slack won't prevent you from feeling light hits.

Tippet Threading Tips

When the fish are rising and your adrenaline is flowing — particularly in failing light conditions — threading the tippet through a small hook eye can be frustrating if your eyesight is not what it used to be. If you have trouble with this, here are several tips that may help.

The use of reading glasses, of course, has long been a standard method for threading a leader through a small eye. And it should go without saying that you should also carry a light to illuminate any knot-tying chores that you may have to perform in low light.

Another good practice is to clip off the end of the leader cleanly with clippers, not bite it off. Besides saving on your dental bills, a clipped leader goes through the eye much easier.

Also, you can now purchase small hooks that have larger eyes for easier tippet threading (I know Orvis, for one, sells these).

Loop-to-Loop Rigging

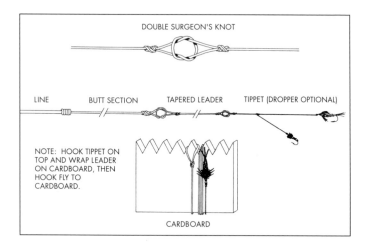

DOUBLE SURGEON'S KNOT

LINE   BUTT SECTION   TAPERED LEADER   TIPPET (DROPPER OPTIONAL)

NOTE: HOOK TIPPET ON TOP AND WRAP LEADER ON CARDBOARD, THEN HOOK FLY TO CARDBOARD.

CARDBOARD

There are also several gadgets on the market that are designed to help you thread tippet through the hook eye. I understand these gadgets work pretty well, but of course they won't do you any good if you don't practice ahead of time at home in a dark room.

If you think you have a good idea what flies may work for you on your upcoming fishing trip, it is a sensible practice in advance of your trip to tie your small flies to tippet sections or two-fly indicator rigs (even using a magnifying light if necessary), and then wind the tippet sections onto a piece of cardboard cut to fit into an empty fly box or your fly wallet. Some anglers take this practice one step further by constructing loops in all their fly/tippet sections, as well as to the end of the leader connected to the fly line, so all they have to do at streamside is to loop the two sections together, which is quite easy to do in failing light or even darkness.

READING THE WATER

The ability to read water is another intellectual exercise that profoundly influences your fishing success. If you can distinguish between water types that hold trout, you will also be able to determine what kind of presentation would be best for that type of water and spend less time fishing over dead water. Of course, there are some trout who reside in the same small habitat year-round, and never move. But depending upon a huge number of variables — the availability of food, the barometer, the weather, the light conditions, the water temperature, the appearance of predators, the fishing pressure, etc., many trout move, and move frequently. Therefore, I find it helpful, whenever I come to new water that I have not fished before, to try to think like a trout and ask myself a series of questions: If I were a trout, what kind water would I feed in today? Would I feed in a riffle, a run, a pool, a flat, a slick, a slough, or a seam? And would I feed deep or shallow?, and so on. Once you can recognize water that feeding trout prefer, your success rate will increase as will your fishing fun.

Riffles — are rapid, shallow, choppy water that holds lots of trout in some watersheds. Because the oxygen level is high, insects and other foods abound, and the choppy surface makes the trout feel more secure. Trout in riffles often feed in 3 inches to 2 feet of water. So never wade into a riffle until you have first fished it. Small nymphs are extremely productive in riffles. Using either the two-fly indicator rig or a standard strike indicator, the usual technique is to present the fly on a natural drift, but swinging the fly in front of a fish sometimes gets its attention better. Of course, your dry-fly pattern should be a good floater, such as a Humpy, to stay up in the choppy water. When the naturals are present, emerger imitations are extremely effective here. There is also spawning substrate in riffles.

Runs — which generally range from 1 to 8 feet in depth — are the somewhat deeper water sections below riffles or rapids that contain moderate currents. They are productive holds for trout because they contain an abundant food supply, and their depth gives the fish a sense of security. When there is not much insect activity in the riffles, trout move back into the runs where they don't have to expend much energy to rest and feed. All stages of insect imitation can be used in this water. Streamers are often effective here.

Pools — which can be from 3 to 40 feet deep — are the deepest part of the stream. This deep, slow water frequently holds the largest trout in the stream, but most of the trout in pools are there to rest, not to feed. The exceptions are the current edges and eddies along the banks or at the sides of pools, and behind or in front of big, submerged rocks. The best technique for fishing the center of a pool is to use a deep two-fly nymphing rig with a strike indicator. For fish holding around rocks or current edges, employ shallow-water techniques.

Flats — On larger rivers, below deep pools you will frequently encounter wide flats with a depth of from 1 to 5 feet and a current flow somewhat faster than that of a pool. These flats are good spots for trout to chase minnows or feed on spent insects. The fish here can be spooky. A bad cast or noisy wading can put them down immediately. It's good water for fishing mini-streamers, small nymphs, dry flies and spinners. At times it is good emerger water.

Slicks — which generally have a depth of from 6 inches to 3 feet — are the shallow, flat areas above riffles. Here you will encounter very selective and spooky trout, which means the use of long, light leaders and delicate, accurate presentations. This can be the most challenging and enjoyable fly fishing on the river. The most effective patterns are small nymphs and spent-wing adults.

Sloughs — which can be from 1 to 12 feet deep — are old side channels or spring inlets that have little water flow. Large trout like to cruise in this water, and delicate presentations are necessary. Sloughs should be fished like ponds. Strike indicators will work here if there is any current at all, and strikes will generally be feather-light. Set the hook on any twitch.

Seams — A current seam, which is a transition area between fast and slow water, is one of the most important trout habitats, but also one of the hardest to deal with because of its varying currents. Trout like to hold in a seam because it is comfortable water, but yet they are close enough to the main channel of the river to quickly dart out and intercept foods that go by in the faster current. When casting into a seam from the shoreline, to get a decent drift, your line, leader, strike indicator, and fly all need to be moving at the same speed in the current. That means some fancy line-mending techniques at times. Fishing seams from a boat is often easier, because you can cast down and across along the current edges and just drift along with your fly. If the water is not too deep, you can also employ this technique while wading. Make a cast across or down and across, and allow your fly to drift along the seam with lots of slack line. Current seams exist in all water types, from rapids to lakes.

Lakes — For most fly fishermen, reading lakes is harder than reading streams, because the currents are not usually visible and the bottom structure is harder to see. But lakes become much easier to read if you divide the lake into sections. The shallow zones, which consist of weedbeds and shallow shelves, are the most productive areas for fly fishermen. The sun can penetrate the depths of the lake here and produce lots of food which will attract trout, especially during insect movements in the morning and evening. At mid-day the trout will likely move deeper and feed better along the outer edges of weedbeds, in the saddles between points, and around channels near inlets, outlets and side canyons.

There are also trout out in the middle of the lake, in deep water, but they are spread out and difficult to cover with a fly. Concentrate more on points, channels, weedbeds, the outer edges of weedbeds, saddles, shelves and the drift lanes (scum lines) when the wind is blowing. The more fish-holding structures you can find, the better the chance that you will find where the trout are and discover the best presentation technique to use.

Lakes can be fished from shore when the trout are in the shallow water looking for nymphs and minnows. Stalk waters where you can see the bottom or along cruising lanes where you suspect trout may be. Cruising lanes are the usual swimming lanes where fish travel, looking for food. Casting to and intercepting trout in cruising lanes is often very productive. Once you find one of these narrow cruising lanes, you should have more confidence fishing small flies here than in the larger body of the lake. A small strike indicator several feet above the fly helps in detecting light hits. The fly should be fished on the sink with an ultra-slow retrieve. When fishing on the sink, if the fly sinks without being intercepted, strip in a few feet of line and allow it to sink again. Moving the fly helps to catch the trout's eye, but moving it too fast in shallow water can spook the fish.

Electronic fish finders are not used very much by fly fishermen, but those who do use them can follow trout movement in lakes. Fish finders can be attached to float tubes and kick boats as well as regular boats. The most valuable type of fish finder for fly rodders is the new side-finder type, which shoots the transducer signal sideways instead of straight down. This feature allows you to find concentrations of trout in shallow water, and by slowly rotating the transducer, you can even find out in which direction the fish are swimming. Finding what areas of the lake trout prefer will also provide you with information about their feeding behavior. For example, if fish are in the shallows but not breaking the surface, they are feeding on insect nymphs, scuds, or leeches.

I am aware some anglers believe that using fish finders is unsportsmanlike, but a fish finder cannot catch fish; it is really just another angling educational tool. Even if you know exactly where the fish are, you still have to catch them on your own.

CONCENTRATING ON THE STRIKE ZONE

You will recall we discussed the importance of strike zones earlier in the book in the chapter on trout feeding behavior. The strike zone behavior that the trout are exhibiting on a given day of fishing should influence the planning of the presentations you will be making that day.

A strike zone is the distance a trout will travel to intercept a fly. While strike zones come in many sizes, they are all roughly peanut-shaped. A "normal" strike zone may be roughly the size of a beach ball. A very large strike zone might be the size of a motor home. Smaller strike zones could be the size of a football, an orange, or even a dime. Selective feeding behavior is often no more than an indication that the trout is utilizing a small strike zone. Your task, in such a case, is to put your fly into that small strike zone with a proper drift.

The strike zone will vary with individual fish on different days and even at different times of the same day. Yet sometimes it remains constant and unvarying for many fish for long periods of time. How many times have you heard, "You should have been here yesterday?" Take the hint. Perhaps the strike zone was big yesterday but today it is smaller. That should tell you to concentrate on putting your fly right on the fish's nose with a good drift. When the strike zone is small, a fish will still eat, *it just won't move to eat*. So, since no fly you present outside the strike zone is likely to be eaten, it's really a waste of time to be making presentations that fall outside the strike

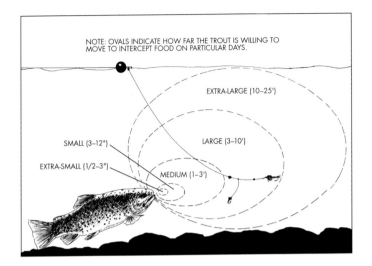

NOTE: OVALS INDICATE HOW FAR THE TROUT IS WILLING TO MOVE TO INTERCEPT FOOD ON PARTICULAR DAYS.

EXTRA-LARGE (10–25')

LARGE (3–10')

SMALL (3–12")

EXTRA-SMALL (1/2–3")

MEDIUM (1–3')

Strike Zones

zone. And if you cannot determine the size of the strike zone, it makes good sense — at least to me — to assume it is a very small one, perhaps no larger than a dime, so that all your casts should attempt to achieve dime-sized presentation accuracy. If it happens that the strike zone is larger, then so much the better. In this case, your dime-sized accurate cast is going to produce just as good results as it would have falling in a landing area as large as a motor home.

For example, when fishing is slow, the trout are generally still feeding, but usually in a small strike zone. That's where your fly has to be. You need to imagine the trout holding in a certain run, to then estimate the size of their strike zone, and to then use whatever presentation technique is necessary to put the fly into that exact area.

Some anglers have an aversion, I think, to presenting flies in a small strike zone. Because this usually means almost bumping the trout in the nose with their fly, they unconsciously think they are getting into some sort of snagging technique. But trout are seldom snagged by accurate, natural presentations. (If they don't like the fly in their strike zone they will move aside and let the fly pass by.) Actually, it is usually a swung fly that snags trout.

ACHIEVING THE PROPER FLY DRIFT LEVEL

The fly drift level is the depth in the water column at which you think the fish are feeding, and at which you decide to present your flies. For example, you can present a fluttering adult pattern that just skims the surface without the hook even touching the water, or a heavily weighted nymph that drags the bottom, or some other pattern at any level between those two extremes. For the sake of this discussion, let's break down the drift levels in the water column into four sections: the surface film (which has three sub-levels); the level extending below the surface down to a depth of about 18 inches; the middle level; and the bottom level of the stream.

Surface Film and Its Three Sub-Levels

The most important but least understood aspect of fly drift level in the water column is the half-inch above and below the actual surface layer of the water. The surface of the water is sort of rubbery. This characteristic is referred to as "surface tension" or the "meniscus." The surface tension prevents hatching insects from leaving the water until they have penetrated this layer. Trout take advantage of this phenomenon by feeding on insects struggling in three levels of the surface film: *just under, right in,* or *just above* it; or, expressing it another way, *sub-surface, transi-*

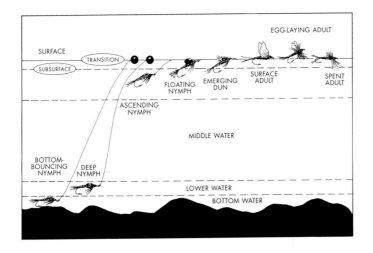

Fly Drift Levels (Mayfly)

tional, and *surface*. They will get keyed in on one of these three levels and will often ignore food anywhere else. Virtually the same foods are being eaten at each level, chosen by the trout based on its past experience, the ease of feeding there, where the food is most highly concentrated, and where it is easiest to feed. This is truly selective feeding behavior.

I've often watched pods of feeding trout in a hatch. Three trout can line up head-to-tail without interfering with each other, and yet one is taking adult insects on the surface, one is taking emergers in the surface film, and one is taking nymphs struggling just under the surface! When you're fishing into such a situation and constantly getting refusals, it's not so much that the fish are refusing your fly; they are simply feeding in a completely different universe than the one your fly is traveling in.

To be a successful small fly angler, it is critical that you understand this important behavioral characteristic of trout. Once you do, you will be able to make effective presentations in any one of the three surface film levels you choose, simply by using a fly pattern that imitates the appropriate insect life-form stage for each level.

The last 10 or 15 years have seen a surge in the development of exact "hatch-imitating" fly patterns designed to imitate certain insects at various life-form stages. This can be a great advantage, assuming that you are able to imitate the life-form stage the trout are keyed in on.

But if you don't know what insect life-form stage the trout are keyed in on, then it might be better practice to try a suggestive pattern or attractor pattern to stimulate the trout to feed on something completely different.

And wouldn't you imagine your success rate would go up if you imitated two suspected favorite food items at the same time? That is why the two-fly indicator rig is so effective. You can narrow down your fly selections twice as fast and cover twice the water.

The Water Level Below the Surface Down to 18 Inches

The two-fly indicator rig also allows you to fish most effectively in the next lower level down in the water column, the level from 1 to 18 inches below the surface. Here is where trout often suspend themselves, eating ascending nymphs and other sunken edibles. They may not even feed on the upper layers near the surface film. In slow water, for example, trout have a long time to look at flies and can afford to be choosy on floating edibles, but are generally not as picky on well-drifted nymphs presented to them a bit lower in the water column. Such patterns represent "safe" foods that anglers don't often imitate properly. If weight is used on the flies in this level of water, it seldom needs to be much. A small amount on the fly itself, or the smallest bit of micro-split shot on the leader, is all that is ever needed. Any weight heavier than that will generally drown the surface fly (if you're using a two-fly indicator rig) or completely sink a strike indicator. In very shallow water, no weight should be used unless you want to fish right along the bottom.

The trout's cone of vision allows it to see more the deeper from the surface it swims. If you place a fly right next to the trout, but out of its strike zone, it will ignore it. But just under the surface a fly enters the trout's cone of vision easier than a fly at its same level.* So as long as the trout's strike zone includes the water several inches under the surface, suspended nymphs will produce well there. But, the trout will not feed on suspended edibles unless there is enough food to make it worth his effort.

The Middle Water

Between the surface layers and the very bottom layers is the middle water. Middle water seldom has a lot of trout feeding activity, unless the trout are aggressively using large strike zones and there is an abundance of ascending nymphs. Regrettably, this is the water level into which most inexperienced fly fishermen place their nymphs. If you have not gained confidence in your nymphing skills, it may very well be because your nymphs are not being fished at the right depth in the water column.

The Bottom Water

The best place to fish nymphs is in the several inches above the bottom of the stream. On all streams, there is a natural drift of aquatic insects that occurs along the stream

---

*See a companion volume in Lefty's Little Library of Fly Fishing, *Fly Fishing for Trout, Volume II,* by Goddard and Clarke, for a complete review of the trout's vision.

bottom, particularly in the morning and evening, as apparently insects seem to be light-sensitive and prefer moving in low-light situations. In the winter, insect movement might be condensed into the middle of the day due to the low angle of the sun. Of course, insects can be found drifting in the water column at any time of day, but nymph imitations are especially effective during early morning and late evening times.

During non-hatch periods, or at the time just before hatches, trout come to rely on nymphs. It has been demonstrated many times that 90 percent of a trout's diet is subsurface food; and that percentage increases to between 98 and 100 percent for larger trout and for trout of all sizes during the winter months. Obviously, if you ignore nymphs in favor of emergers and dry flies, you are severely limiting your chances for success.

To fish the deeper water near the bottom effectively, a floating line with a two-fly indicator rig, or a nymph rig with a strike indicator, are the preferred rigs. Sinking lines are used mainly for swung or retrieved flies, but they are really impossible to work with on selective trout with small, naturally drifted flies. This is because with a sinking line you must keep a tight line to feel the strike, and that precludes being able to achieve a natural drift with one. Because — excepting those situations when you are fishing streamers and some pupa imitations in which a moving wet fly would be a natural sight to the trout — if you place enough slack in a sinking line to achieve a natural drift, then you cannot detect hits. On most trout streams, for any naturally drifted nymph presentation you are trying to make, the floating line is really the only way to go. A floating line can be mended and adjusted to

Dory fishing at Kong's Bed, Green River, Utah. ▶

achieve a relatively natural drift, and the leader is affected less by the currents than it would be on a sinking line.

If you use a strike indicator, it needs to be buoyant enough to support the weight of the fly and whatever weight you have added without being too bulky or wind-resistant. A long, light tippet sinks best and is easiest to keep floating drag-free, but alas, it does not turn over weighted flies very well on the cast. Luckily, with small flies, there is less air resistance and long tippets are easier to use.

Using the proper amount of weight is critical for natural drift down in the bottom zone of the water column. Too much weight and your flies will drag along the bottom of the stream (and also makes your casting difficult). Too little weight and you will not get your flies down into the strike zone before the drift is entirely over.

Weight can be added to the pattern itself with a weighted underbody or with lead eyes. A better method of weighting, however, is the use of split shot on the leader. The best combination of weights that I have found is micro-split shot together with removable size B and BB split shot. The micro-shot — usually one with enough weight to provide the fly with a natural drift in water up to 2 feet deep — should be placed several inches from the fly. If you cannot keep tension out of the line, you will also need more weight to get down. But in deeper water the micro-shot will not get the job done. Then you should attach a larger (size B or BB) removable weight to the leader 1 to 2 feet from the fly. If there is a dropper off the leader, place the main weight several inches above it.

This method of weighting is quite versatile. In shallow water, just use the micro-shot. As the water deepens or current speed picks up, add more weight with the removable BBs. To know if you have the right amount of weight on, concentrate on what the strike indicator is telling you.

If it is drifting along with the current, your nymph is probably not deep enough.

If it is drifting at a rate slightly slower than the surface currents, great! You are in the strike zone. If it keeps hanging up on the bottom, remove some weight. The idea is to keep the nymph within several inches of the stream bottom without dragging constantly.

In addition to weight, you must cast far enough upstream to allow the nymph time to sink before it reaches the strike zone. Flies sink faster, with less weight needed, if the drift is natural. Flies that land downstream of the strike indicator sink faster than flies that curl out straight up and across from the indicator, but you must make sure the flies are under or behind the strike indicator before they reach the strike zone or you may miss strikes.

ACHIEVING NATURAL DEAD-DRIFT

Regarding presentation, natural dead-drift is what separates the experts from the amateurs. Natural dead-drift imitates what natural insects are doing on the water. (It should not be confused with the dead-drift technique that many steelhead or salmon anglers use, in which the fly is swung in the current with no retrieve or other action imparted to the fly.)

Drag is what happens when the current acts on the line or leader and pulls the fly from the position in which it should naturally be. The most insidious type of drag is referred to as "micro-drag," which is the minute, almost invisible drag that you cannot easily see but which the trout can see because it is so much closer to the fly.

It should be mentioned here that it's almost impossible to get a perfectly natural, drag-free drift, because of all the varying factors — currents, wind, obstructions, etc. — that can influence the fly's action on the water. But unnatural drag — particularly micro-drag — is the biggest problem in fishing small flies properly, perhaps even the principal reason for fly rejection, and one of the fly fisherman's greatest enemies.

Unless you always fish for uneducated trout, small flies simply cannot be fished effectively without learning how to eliminate as much drag from your presentation as possible, and to achieve as natural a drift as possible. But as I have discussed before, with the pressure that is being focused on many trout streams today, finding uneducated trout is getting harder and harder.

So what are the factors that contribute to presenting flies on a dead-drift that the educated and catch-and-release trout will respond to?

First, of course, are all the casting, mending, and line management techniques that we are discussing throughout this book.

It is also important that you are fishing with a properly constructed leader. If your leader is all kinked up, it will lengthen as you cast it and then contract after it hits the water, like a spring, causing the fly to drag even if the line itself has no actual drag. So always make sure your leader is straightened, and use a long, limp tippet for best results.

Next is to keep in mind that a natural dead-drift is not possible with a tight line. Enough slack in the line or leader, or both, must be introduced to create a situation for the fly to drift without drag. The idea is not to have a straight leader, but to have one that will stay in the general shape that you or the current gives it so as not to pull the fly from where it should naturally be. The leader itself needs to be soft enough to allow it to interact freely with the natural twists and turns of the currents. A leader that is too stiff will pull the fly from its original position. That is the main reason for going to lighter tippets, not because the trout cannot see the fine tippets (I'm convinced that trout can see all leaders and tippets anyway). C & R trout, for example, may not be particularly bothered by the sight of a leader on the water, but they will almost always be put down by a dragging fly.

SMALL FLY LINE MANAGEMENT, MENDING AND CASTING TECHNIQUES FOR DEAD-DRIFT PRESENTATIONS

Of course, casting is the foundation of all fly-fishing technique, and for all practical purposes, all the casting techniques you have acquired apply equally well to large and small flies. But since casting has been superbly covered by Lefty in several companion books in this Library, I will not be covering that ground again here.*

However, I do have a few tips about small fly casting, as well as line management and line mending with small fly presentations, that I think are worth examining.

Line Management

Line management is one of the most important aspects of achieving natural drift. If you watch a fly fisherman who is good at fishing for selective trout, you will also see

---

*For comprehensive discussions of fly casting, see these volumes in Lefty's Little Library of Fly Fishing: *Lefty Kreh's Modern Fly Casting Method; Lefty's Little Tips* (pp. 133-141); *Fly Fishing Techniques and Tactics* (pp. 93-123); *Fly Fishing for Trout, Volume I* (pp. 152-157); and *American Masters Fly Fishing Symposium, Volume I* (pp. 123-155).

someone who is constantly adjusting his casting, mending, and line management techniques to suit the immediate situation. There is no single, absolute formula that always works for good line management. Each place you fish and each angle of your cast require you to manage your line and adjust your presentation to achieve the best natural drift possible.

Mending

Mending is the act of flipping the line with the rod tip in a direction other than the normal cast dictated. A mend can be done during the cast (called an "in-the-air" or "reach" mend). Many other types of mends can be used to compensate for currents after the cast is completed. Too many mends, or mends in the wrong direction, can be worse than no mends at all. *Knowing when and how to mend is essential to fishing small flies naturally.*

Casting

The average angler usually makes a standard or traditional cast up and across the stream. As the fly drifts down opposite the angler, he mends upstream and then lets the fly drift down naturally until it starts dragging downstream. But unless this technique just so happens to be the best way to present a particular fly on a particular day in that particular situation, this is not the presentation that the experienced small fly angler would use.

To understand this, let's examine the types of presentations that can be made, which are really defined by the casting angles or directions that the angler can utilize on a stream (direction being the linear relationship between the angler and the spot where the fly lands). There are five: *straight upstream, up-and-across stream, across stream, down-and-across stream,* and *straight downstream.*

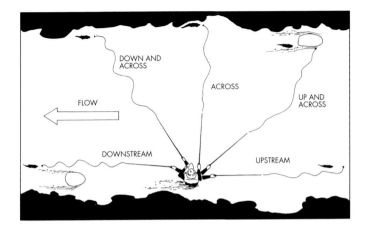

Angle of Presentation

The **straight-upstream cast** is valuable for fishing up-stream to pocket water, because the fast water associated with pocket water often disguises from the fish the impact of the leader and fly on the water. It can also be used to fish along the bank or along rocks that break the current. It is not a good cast for flat water, because the leader (and with a bad presentation also the line) will land on the water directly and noticeably above the trout, usually putting the fish down.

Mending on an upstream cast is best accomplished by a reach mend. The reach mend is made by casting toward a secondary target upstream of the fish (remember the trout is your primary target).

To determine the secondary target, visualize where the trout is (or might be) and then choose a spot in a direct line upstream from the trout where the impact of your fly on the water would not likely spook the trout. That is your secondary target. After the casting stroke is made but before the line hits the water, smoothly move the rod one

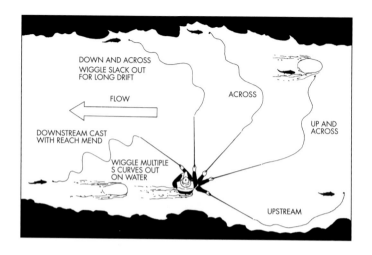

DOWN AND ACROSS
WIGGLE SLACK OUT
FOR LONG DRIFT

FLOW

ACROSS

UP AND
ACROSS

DOWNSTREAM CAST
WITH REACH MEND

WIGGLE MULTIPLE
S CURVES OUT
ON WATER

UPSTREAM

Reach Mends/Slack Mends for Natural Drift

way or the other so that when the fly lands on that secondary target, the fly line is positioned at an angle to you, but the fly is straight upstream from the fish. When you are fishing dry flies in fast pocket water, the secondary target could be just a foot or two upstream of the fish. In shallow, clear, flat water, it could be as much as 15 or 20 feet upstream of the trout.

If you are nymph fishing, you may need to select secondary targets even further upstream, as nymphs require more distance and time to sink deeply into the water column to the proper drift level before reaching the trout's holding position.

When an in-the-air or reach mend is made, it is best to let a little line slip through your fingers and allow it to slip through the rod guides to compensate for the extra rod movement that was created by the mend. Otherwise the fly will bounce back, away from your intended target. It takes practice to do this, but the reach mend is the most valuable mend that the angler can learn. It allows you to position the line better without moving yourself or having to mend after the line hits the water. Often it is the only mend you need for a good drift.

It's obvious, I suppose, that you need some degree of angle between you and the fish to make an effective reach mend. If you are in a position directly downstream of the fish, casting directly upstream, you cannot create the necessary angle between you and your fly to create a good drift. If you find yourself in that position, it would be best to move, if possible. But if you cannot do that, it is better just to strip in line, or raise the rod, to deal with slack coming back towards you.

The **up-and-across-stream cast** is most often used for presenting flies to rising or nymphing trout when casting from a bank or when casting from shallow water towards faster water. There are various types of mends that can be utilized with this cast.

Again, the reach mend is the most valuable. Cast up and across and deliver an upstream reach mend. This positions the line almost 90 degrees to the stream bank, even though the fly is 45 degrees from the angler. After the fly hits the water, drop the rod to create slack and allow a natural drift.

Or, if you want the fly to drift below your position on the river, make an on-the-water mend if necessary, and immediately let more slack out on the water. This additional slack line will allow the fly to drift to a down-and-across position before it starts to swing.

This type of presentation allows you to achieve a drift as long or longer than the length of the cast. Without employing these mends, the fly would not drift naturally for more than a few feet, unless, of course, there were perfect currents (which is rare).

When casting across slow water towards faster water, the mend needs to be different. I'm talking about situations in which you encounter a drastic difference in current speeds between your position in the water and the main current or its seams and eddy lines where you wish to place your fly. If you cast straight up and across, you would almost immediately get drag, as the varying currents will be acting on the line and leader differently. The solution is to maneuver your line, leader, and fly into the same current speed. The best way to accomplish this is to cast up and across, make a downstream reach mend that throws the line into the same current speed as the fly, then introduce enough slack line to allow a natural drift. Additional mends should be made downstream and out towards the faster current. This method is particularly effective for strike indicator nymph fishing. If you are casting across the current seam to fish the faster water itself, you will need to make an upstream reach mend (to position the line best for the fast water), then a downstream, on-the-water mend to position the line closer to you for a drag-free drift.

The **across-stream cast** is one of the best devices for making presentations to selective trout or for fishing to the pocket water behind boulders in fast water. If you can wade or float-fish the main river and cast towards shore, you can pick up bank feeders this way. Here again, you need to determine if an in-the-air mend is appropriate. It usually is. Cast straight across and make an upstream reach mend. That positions the line so the fly is coming down before the line and leader, at about a 45-degree angle from the bank. The longer the cast, the less of an angle there will be, but it is no less important.

When fishing to the pocket water behind big rocks, get close to the target so your cast will not be too far away.

Make the usual cast and upstream mend just before your fly reaches the pocket. Keep the rod higher than normal so the faster current next to the pocket water does not immediately pull the fly away. If needed, make several short controlled mends that actually throw a small pile of slack line upstream of the fly. With slack line upstream of the fly, it will drift downstream naturally.

If you are casting toward the slow water next to shore from a boat or when wading, the across-stream cast with an upstream reach mend is again the best technique to employ; a cast straight across stream will start dragging immediately unless you position the line upstream, because the water next to shore is moving slower than the main current. You may also need to immediately start feeding slack out for a good drift.

The **down-and-across-stream cast** was made popular on the Henry's Fork in Idaho for fishing to selective bank feeders. Traditional casts would drag, and if the trout saw the leader before the fly, it would trigger a non-feeding response until the fly passed. After much trial and error, it was determined that fishing the fly not up, but down to the trout was the best angle of presentation. Casting down and across is a versatile technique. Use it anytime you are fishing towards the bank or in any area where the fly is on slower water than you are in.

The down-and-across cast is also a good technique when making presentations from drift boats, rafts or float tubes. It gets the fly downstream of the boat into water where the trout have not yet been alerted to the presence of the boat. If you are drifting with the current, very little needs to be done in the way of mending with this cast — just keep some slack in the line. If you are wading and casting

OVERLEAF: *Golden trout anglers on the Titcomb Lakes outlet, Utah.*

down and across, it helps to make an upstream reach mend and then immediately begin letting line out.

A variation of this cast can get the fly accurately into the fish's feeding lane even if it's windy or your casts are less than accurate. Cast down and across, beyond the feeding lane of the trout but upstream of its position. Immediately raise the rod gently so the fly is skittering on the water. Keep raising the rod until the fly reaches the trout's feeding lane (preferably several feet above the trout). Then simply drop the rod and let the current carry the fly down naturally to the trout. This technique also works well on trout holding in current edges, seams, and weedy channels; or where the currents are tricky and accurate casting is difficult. It works best with dry flies, but it will also work with the two-fly indicator rig if the tippet to the dropper nymph is fairly short.

Most people think that a down-and-across presentation cannot achieve a long drift, but in reality, it can achieve some of the longest natural drifts possible. The secret is the angler's ability to strip line and wiggle it out of his rod tip. That may sound simple enough, but as a fishing guide, I have found it is one of the most difficult things to teach most clients. Here is why. If you do not let line out before you need it, you will simply start dragging the fly as you begin to let line out. That's no good. Most people begin okay, but continue to mend the line in the usual upstream direction as they wiggle line out. But by this time, the line is drifting downstream but they are mending upsteam, so that a big S-curve develops that immediately begins to exert drag on the fly. Just one S-curve of this sort in the line cannot provide enough slack to keep the fly drifting naturally.

Instead, as you strip line off the reel and wiggle it out of the rod tip, mend in one direction and then the other, gently. This creates multiple S-curves in the line on the water, and sometimes even a small pile of slack below the rod tip, which allows the current to act on the line without dragging the fly. Sometimes full mends may be needed, which will probably move the fly. If so, after each mend be sure to immediately let slack line out again to continue the natural drift.

If you want the longest natural drift you have ever seen, I suggest you practice this down-and-across cast/strip/wiggle technique. Anyone that masters it can get an 80-foot drift if the run is long enough. And from a boat the drift can be even longer. With a drift that long, imagine the water you could fish that other anglers have passed by because they couldn't cover it with their fly! Or imagine drifting a hopper with a small nymph dropper as much as 50 feet down an undercut bank or over drop-offs that cannot be fished from shore! It takes practice but is well worth the effort.

I don't know why it is, but fly rodders seem terrified of slack line. Perhaps it's a natural instinct to believe that you cannot set the hook with slack line; or that slack will cause you to lose control of your fly. Whatever the reason, over and over I see fly fishermen stripping in line immediately after the cast until all slack has been removed. And then they wonder why their fly is dragging! If you've ever been guilty of that practice, I hope you have changed your thinking. Otherwise, when you are fishing to trout who are being selective to drag, you won't have to worry about setting your hook. Keep a tight line and no trout are going to hit! It's better practice to get the right presentation to begin with (which means slack line), and then worry about setting the hook later when the trout does take.

To set the hook with a slack line, lower the rod so it is parallel to the water and set the hook with a side strike, away from the fish. The water pressure almost immediately takes all of the slack line out and assists you in properly setting the hook.

The **straight-downstream cast**, which is used extensively for fishing skittering dry flies, such as egg-laying caddis, is a difficult presentation but has its place in a fly fisherman's bag of tricks. After the cast, raise the rod quickly enough to keep the dry fly skittering on the surface. Then drop the rod tip and the fly will drift down to the trout naturally. Repeat the process and sweep the rod from one side to the other. This will frequently tease up trout feeding on caddis adults, egg-laying midges or craneflies. And the rises are spectacular!

The hard part with this cast is setting the hook properly. A normal hook set will usually pull the fly right out of the fish's mouth. It's best to delay the strike longer than usual. This delay allows the fish to turn down and close its mouth before the hook is set. And then set the hook sidearm, just like the strike you use for a long line with slack. Setting the hook to the side will help the point of the hook find good purchase.

Nymphing downstream is most difficult. It can be done, but it requires that you execute a tuck cast which tucks the fly under the fly line and strike indicator, allowing it to sink straight under the indicator. Slack line is then immediately needed. It's a very effective technique in the right hands, because you can fish water that seldom sees a fly, and you do not need to change your position to fish water below you if you don't want to. But the tuck cast takes practice.*

---

*See a companion volume in Lefty's Little Library of Fly Fishing, *Fly Fishing for Trout, Volume I*, pp. 154-158, for Lefty's demonstration of how to execute the tuck cast.

Once you learn to create natural drifts to trout at the various angles I have described, there are several other points I would like to emphasize.

Since the trout is obviously the primary target, unless you are faced with fish feeding in an extremely small strike zone, your cast should not land on the trout's head, but on a secondary upstream target you have chosen as your casting direction. Nymphs will require choosing a secondary target further upstream than the one you would select for a dry fly.

Do not cast at a rise-form of a surface feeder or the flash of a nymphing trout. If you do, you will be casting on the trout's head or behind it. Determine where the rise-form or flash occurred, and pick your secondary casting target upstream of that point. Of course, if the trout are operating in a small strike zone, accuracy is critical. Sometimes two or three dozen casts to the same area may be required before the fly drifts perfectly into the small strike zone. Usually, however, the first cast or two will be the most critical for success.

As currents change and become more intricate, so must the subtleties of your casts and mends to keep the fly drifting naturally.

SMALL FLY CASTING TECHNIQUES TO GIVE ACTION TO FLIES

Now that I've filled your head with visions of naturally drifting flies, I'm going to talk about those times when you need to purposely give them action. Of course, the reason you would move a fly would be to imitate the action of a natural that moves in the water. Sometimes a moving fly just gets the attention of the trout better than a still fly, or it might even trigger a "think fast" reaction. Whatever the reason, on any given day, it may take a little experimentation to discover if the trout are taking a moving fly better than a stationary imitation.

Sometimes it is as simple as letting the fly swing at the end of the natural drift. In stillwater fishing, as well as when making presentations to imitate ascending pupae, egg-laying insects, streamers, and leeches, action will need to be given to the flies at times.

When an insect hatch is on, there is more movement in the water than the movement of just the insects that are emerging. For example, some insects will swim to the surface several times before they are ready to emerge. Caddis pupae, in particular, are excellent swimmers and they shoot up to the surface very quickly. There is no "dead-drift" about it.

Therefore, when trout are feeding on caddis, caddis pupa patterns can be fished on the swing. Just cast down and across and allow the fly to swing in the current. Take a step or lengthen the line and repeat. It is a simple technique that has worked for hundreds of years with various wet flies. However, it has been my experience that except in late evenings, catch-and-release trout will seldom take a caddis pupa, small minnow, or crayfish imitation on the swing.

When trout want a more natural looking caddis pupa presentation, the drift/rise presentation is better. To do that, cast the fly up and across. Let the weighted fly sink, then raise the rod. This looks like an ascending pupa to the trout. With a little finesse you can make that lift three or four times during a drift. In between rod lifts, watch for trout to take the natural drifting imitation.

The two-fly indicator rig with an Elk-Hair Caddis and a LaFontaine or Palomino Deep Sparkle Pupa tied on a 3 or 4-foot tippet can be a deadly combo for this type fishing. Only a few people I've seen are real masters at the technique, but here's how you do it. As the flies start swinging downstream, keep raising and lowering the rod to skim the dry fly and the pupa up to the surface, then let the rig drift back. The trout may take the dry or the emerger, and the dry fly is always working on the surface as a strike indicator. Generally, trout take the pupal stage more readily than the adult. When caddis are hatching, try pupa imitations naturally drifted and swung up in front of the trout and watch out!

In lakes, swimming motion of the insects is natural and much easier to see than in streams. Trout in lakes more often than not expect to see their insects swimming. A fly with no movement will often be ignored. Exceptions exist, of course, such as when using dry flies or snail imitations, but most lake patterns need to have some sort of action imparted to them.

Sometimes a weighted nymph sinking on a long leader and floating line is all the action that is needed. Use a small strike indicator to help detect light hits. Here is a particularly effective technique when you can see a trout cruising in the shallows. Cast far enough in front of the trout so the nymph has enough time to sink into its strike zone. Watch for movement of the trout that indicates it took your fly. The white of its mouth, a hesitation, a direction change, or a twitch on the leader should tell you to set the hook. Small, unweighted flies can be weighted by using micro-shot on the leader. If casting spooks the trout, cast into a cruising lane before the trout enters the area and let the fly sink to the bottom until the trout comes by. Start a slow strip as the trout nears the fly. The trout will frequently think it is a disturbed nymph and intercept it.

When blind fishing small nymphs in a cruising lane, you want to cover as much water as possible without moving the fly so rapidly that the trout get suspicious. Make sure you are fishing at the right depth. If your fly is up near the surface and the fish are not surface-oriented, you will not have much success. Use the appropriate sinking line or weighted fly for the situation.

If there's a wind, wind drifting small flies can save a slow fishing day. There are two techniques: casting cross-wind from a stationary position, or casting from a drifting boat or float tube. Use a floating line, a strike indicator and a long leader. If you are wading, make a cross-wind cast and allow the wind to move the fly along slowly by letting it gradually blow your line down-wind, creating an ultra-slow presentation that is ideal for small fly work. Also, the wave action created by the wind generally gives a bit of life-like movement to the fly. If you are in a boat, raft, or float tube, let the wind move you and trail the fly behind. Cast to new areas occasionally. This method can cover lots of water, helping you find concentrations of fish; and has the added advantage of reducing the amount of casting you will need to do in the wind.

Scuds, pupae and nymphs are all swimmers in lakes. They swim across channels in weedbeds, up to the surface, then back down and along the bottom. Their action can sometimes be as slow as that of a mayfly; sometimes as fast as that of a caddis pupa. Scuds swim slowly forward or rapidly backwards. On imitations of all these naturals, the retrieve speed on the typical cast should be relatively slow in comparison to the retrieve speeds that are normally used for lake flies. If you are used to fishing larger flies like Woolly Buggers, then you probably will have to concentrate on keeping your retrieve speed slower. Imagine to yourself how long it would take the natural to swim one foot and fish the fly that fast. Short strips often help.

Exceptions are obvious. Sometimes a fast retrieve gets the trout's attention and it reacts by pouncing on the fly. I usually start with a fairly fast retrieve and cover a lot of water. Once I am confident, because of hits or rises, that I am fishing over trout, I begin to experiment with slower, more natural retrieves.

One presentation that often works is that of an ascending nymph. With a floating line and a 12 to 18-foot long leader, cast a weighted nymph and let it sink for a minute or more, being on the alert for strikes all the while. Then start a retrieve and make five or six strips. If nothing hits, let the fly sink again and repeat. Since each retrieve is causing the nymph to rise towards the surface, you are covering different depths in the water column, and you can quickly learn at which depth the trout are feeding.

Small minnow, leech and crayfish imitations can be very effective on the biggest trout in the area. They are often best fished near structures that would attract the foods that attract larger trout. Fish these patterns along reed lines, the deeper edges of weedbeds, rocky shallows (especially in early morning and late evening), submerged reefs and points, and near fallen timber. Fish them fast when you see that the trout are using a large strike zone, and slower and deeper when the strike zone is small.

When the shoreline is steep, fish small flies close to shore by casting towards or parallel to the shore. In areas where the bank is gently sloping, find the right depth and concentrate on that contour. The three things to keep in mind when lake fishing are *location* (where would the fish be concentrated), *level of presentation* (depth) and *imitation* (fly pattern and retrieving style). Location, level of presentation and imitation also happen to be the three things to remember when stream fishing.

A variety of retrieves can be used for fly fishing lakes. They will all work at some time or another. Short and fast, 1 to 2-inch strips will work sometimes and a long, slow, steady strip will work at others. A moderately fast retrieve with occasional pauses will often trigger hits, as when the trout starts following the fly and suddenly it stops and the fly is in its face, the fish will either spook off or eat the fly. Sometimes it will hit the fly on the very first strip after a pause. If your retrieve is not performing to your satisfaction, change and experiment.

In streams, there are times when moving flies work very well, but in heavily fished waters only five percent or less of the feeding trout will respond to a fly activation technique. The natural drift is obviously to be preferred in moving water. In stillwater, the active imitation works best, but don't get yourself into a rigid mind set about this. Observe and experiment.

PLAYING TROUT ON LIGHT TACKLE

Once everything comes together and the trout hits, you need to develop certain skills at playing fish on the light rods, leaders and tippets that you will be employing with small flies. There is a huge difference between playing trout on big hooks and heavy tippets and playing them on small flies and light tippets.

If you use your usual fish fighting techniques, you may break the trout off. Or if you're new to the small fly game and lack confidence in light tackle, you may tend to baby the trout too much and keep it on the rod for an extraordinarily long time. This is bad for the fish, of course, and may be bad for you if the trout breaks you off during all that extra time you gave it.

Setting the hook on small flies is an art. It is usually just a light lift of the rod until the pressure of the fish is felt. Keep moving the rod until the slack is gone and there is a moderate bend in the rod. This should be a firm but not overly aggressive movement. Traditionally, anglers have brought the rod straight up overhead for the hook set.

But nowadays, more and more people are switching to the **side (or side-arm) strike** technique because of several advantages. If the trout takes the fly on a downstream or down-and-across presentation, a hook set straight up will often be pulled right out of its mouth; whereas a side strike gets an assist from the current to help pull the fly into the corner of the trout's mouth, where it will hook better. Or from a boat, it will keep the fly from hooking your oarsman if you miss the fish. Or if you are fishing a brushy stream, it will assist you in setting the hook in a direction so that your rod tip or line will not snag on vegetation. Sometimes that means setting the hook with the rod tip just inches from the water. In a tight situation like this, you can use a small side strike.

Or, you can elect to use a **strip (or line) strike**. On the strip strike, the rod is moved very little during the striking action. At hook-setting time, simply make a big strip — big enough to remove all the slack out of your line — with your line hand, and put the hook home. Sometimes more than one strip strike may be needed.

Or, you can elect to use the **slip strike**. The slip strike has gained lots of attention in the last few years since small flies have become more popular. It is accomplished by setting the hook normally, but letting some line slip through your fingers during the striking process. This helps protect light tippets from breakage, and in addition leaves you ready to let more line slip through your fingers should the trout immediately bolt away. If you don't use the slip strike, you need to consciously change your strike powering when you switch to smaller hook sizes and lighter tippet strengths. But this should not cost you fish. Most people don't realize how strong modern hooks and the newer tippet materials are. To check this out for yourself, conduct Lefty's test: tie some new 5X or 6X-tippet to a door knob or table leg (with a properly tied knot) and lean back on the rod. You will be amazed at how much pressure you can put on such a light tippet with a steady pull. You may not even be able to break it. But if you rapidly accelerate the rod or put jerks on the line, of course, it will break very easily. Too fast a hook set actually creates shock waves that bounce back and forth between the rod and the fly, often popping a delicate tippet. But striking too slowly may lose the fish. Work out a happy medium that feels right to you.

Side and slip strikes are also helpful in avoiding fish break-offs. Generally after a hook-up, a trout will jump or thrash wildly. When that happens, many anglers either freeze up or try to muscle the trout. For their pains they may get a break-off, a bent hook, or a broken tippet — particularly on big fish. I've found the best train of thought for this first few seconds of the fight is "set the hook and let it run." The instant you set the hook, also be ready to let slack line slip through your fingers if the trout runs. If the trout does not run immediately, get control of your slack line and reel it up on the reel, but always be ready to let the trout run again. Once you get the trout on the reel, quickly remove your hand from the handle anytime the fish starts to run. Don't try to back-reel, you cannot keep up with a fast trout.

If the trout jumps, drop the rod down towards the water and let go of the reel handle at the same time so that some slack line will be available to absorb the shock of the jump. Immediately raise the rod after the fish re-enters the water, then grab the reel handle again, but not before. If the trout bolts while you are pointing the rod at the fish and holding onto the reel, there is a good chance of breaking the fish off. For most trout fighting on small flies, angle the rod grip vertically (90 to 45 degrees) to maintain shock-absorbing power in the rod. Holding the rod at any lower angle will be asking for a break-off, especially if you are holding onto the reel handle. A rod handle held at 90 degrees from the vertical has the best shock absorbing tendencies and at 45 degrees from the vertical it has the best power for moving stubborn fish.

On light tackle, you want the bend of the fly rod and the stretch of the leader and line to be your principal shock absorbers. As soon as that shock absorption is nullified, the trout will break off. Keep in mind, too, that with the exception of the new non or low-stretch lines, most 90-foot fly lines have as much as 15 feet of stretch. Tapered monofilament leaders can stretch several inches to a foot or more. This is a lot of shock-absorbing capacity, more than most anglers realize.

Of course, leaders and tippets still break regularly. But such breaks seldom come from rod movement. The principal cause is poor technique on the part of the angler — a poorly tied knot, failure to regularly examine the leader for nicks, poor casting technique that places wind knots in the tippet, not allowing the trout to run when it wants to, and so on.

A bent or broken hook point, a bent hook-bend, a barbless hook, a barbed hook that has not penetrated properly, or a hook that has failed to penetrate much flesh, can all easily come loose. Check hooks and tippets regularly for damage, especially after releasing or losing a trout, or hitting rocks or branches with the hook or leader.

A trout that gets downstream of the angler and thrashes is likely to pop the hook out, especially with barbless hooks. Using an appropriate rod angle can help land fish quickly, without losing the trout or breaking it off. Try to keep the angle of the fly line at 90 degrees or less in relation to the trout. A trout that gets too far downstream can cause problems because it instinctively knows how to use current to its advantage. But if you can maintain a position even with the trout's position in the stream, or even below it, you have the advantage because you can keep the trout off balance and coming towards you. This will result in landing the trout quicker, which is better for the trout, and landing more trout, which is better for you.

You don't always need to wade or walk down the shoreline to achieve an efficient rod angle. Depending upon the fish's position in the stream, lean your rod upstream or downstream and you have immediately gained a 7 or 8-foot advantage. Holding the rod at a low angle parallel to the water is harder for the trout to deal with. A stubborn trout can be "walked" towards you by holding your rod low and repeatedly changing the rod angle from one side to another while applying pressure at each angle to keep the trout zig-zagging towards you; whereas if you hold your rod high and at just one angle, you are giving the trout a great opportunity to rest in the current and regain its strength. But don't just mechanically swing the rod upstream and then down, do it with purpose. Try to accomplish something with each rod angle change you make.

Landing trout can be difficult on light tippets and small flies. This is where most trout are lost, in the second half of the fight. Nets are sometimes used for increasing the speed of landing trout in difficult positions, such as from a drift boat or when you are hip-deep in the middle of a river. Nets are also used for insuring that a large trout is landed for a picture. But most anglers are staying away from nets now, which is a good thing, I think. A net is pretty tough on a trout. Regardless of the net's material, as the trout thrashes inside the mesh, it can remove a substantial portion of the trout's natural slime that protects it from diseases — just as if you had scrubbed the trout's back with a wash cloth. An expert with net releases takes little time with the trout in the net, but most anglers actually increase handling time when they attempt to land and release trout with a net.

There is an art to landing and releasing trout quickly and healthily. To land a trout on light tippets without a net, play the trout in as quickly as you can without breaking the fish off. A trout played too long will take a long time to revive. Leave the fish in deeper water in the stream until you are all set to make your landing move. If you permit the fish to remain in shallow warm water along the shore for a long time, this increases the harmful build-up of lactic acid in the fish, because it cannot obtain oxygen from warm water nearly as well as it can from the cooler water in the middle of the stream.

When the trout calms down sufficiently, lead it in to slow water and grab the fly with your hemostats for removal. Push down to release the barb, then back the hook out with one quick motion, the way it went in. If you grab the lower part of the hook bend, the fly will come out easiest, with or without a barb on the hook.

It has been generally accepted wisdom in the fly-fishing world that barbless hooks are best. Some recent studies have shown that there is little difference in trout mortality between barbed and barbless hooks, or even barbed treble hooks. But there is now also evidence contrary to the "barbless is best" rule. We are learning that a barbless hook can penetrate a trout's mouth more deeply and with multiple penetrations at the same entry point in its flesh (this is called the "stiletto effect"), whereas a barb tends to hold the hook point in place and avoid such multiple penetrations. Barbless hooks also often jump around inside a trout's mouth during the fight, making wounds in several locations. Small barbless hooks can also cut a jagged incision in the trout's tender mouth parts, such as the roof of its mouth. But, the wound caused by a barbed hook is generally superficial and not really damaging.

The jury's still out on this question, I suppose. There are no hard and fast moral rules anymore about whether you should or should not go barbless. The real reasons for going barbless, it seems to me, is that it protects you and your fishing companions from serious hook wounds; or, of course, that fishing barbless has become a legal requirement on some waters.

There is no doubt that novice anglers can reduce handling time through the use of barbless hooks, because they obviously do come out easier. Removing a barbed hook from a fish is actually pretty easy, however, if you will take the time to learn how to do it properly. If you have trouble grasping a barbed fly, lean the trout against your leg and run the hemostats down the leader to the hook or grab the trout's lower jaw between your thumb and forefinger — unless it's a big critter with big teeth — for better control. If the trout has the fly embedded down its throat or in its gills, simply cut the leader. It's better to sacrifice one fly for a trout than one trout for a fly. Also, small flies generally do less damage than big flies, regardless of whether you decide to fish barbless or not.

You do not even need to touch a trout, unless it needs reviving. If you do need to pick up a trout, there are several things you can do to minimize stress. First of all, hold it over water so that if you drop it, the fish won't be injured by the impact with the bank or the bottom of a boat. Small trout can be held gently upside down, cradled in your hand, and will seldom struggle. Never squeeze a trout, whatever its size.

Large trout — which are the ones that are the most photographed — should never be held with one hand. Their internal organs are used to a weightless environment, and the simple act of raising the trout out of the water can cause damage. If you want a picture of a large trout, get the camera ready before taking the trout out of the water. Get into position and then raise the trout out of the water gently with two hands, one holding the small of the trout's tail and the other gently cradling the head and belly, near its front fins. Don't keep a trout out of the water for longer than you can hold your breath after a jog.

To revive the fish, hold its lower jaw open slightly with your thumb or forefinger, in moderate to slow current. This method of reviving can speed up the trout's recovery. Don't release the trout until you are sure that it has gained back sufficient strength, especially in hot weather.

Since I know you are going to catch more trout with small flies, I think it's a fair deal for you to take on the responsibility of learning how to handle them properly, don't you?

OVERLEAF: *Dave Larson holding a nice rainbow caught on a scud, Provo River, Utah.*

CHAPTER FIVE

LIGHT TACKLE FOR SMALL FLIES

It's pretty obvious, I suppose, that tackle for fishing small flies will be on the lighter or smaller end of the tackle spectrum. That does not mean that you cannot be successful fishing small flies on heavyweight gear. Of course you can. Any combination of fishing tackle that can get the fly over the fish sufficiently well to fool it into a take has to be regarded as effective. But if you decide to devote a fair amount of your time to fishing to trout with small flies — which I hope you will — there are lighter and smaller tackle components that will do the job better and more comfortably.

Rods

Take rods for example. The nature of small fly fishing suggests that rod line weights be kept fairly light. You can fish a #18 dry fly on an 8-weight rod, but a 4-weight would be more comfortable and more fun to fish. Line weights from 1 to 7 constitute the range of the most effective small fly rods. Some people fish 1-weight rods, but they are really toys, not high performance fishing instruments. But 2 and 3-weight rods are very popular for fishing midges and other micro-patterns. There is now available a good selection of commercial rods in these light weights. For nymphing in larger rivers or lakes, or for casting in windy conditions, use 4 to 7-weight rods.

One thing to consider in selecting a lightweight rod is the presentation aspect of the various fly line weights. Lighter lines are generally more limp, and can reduce the amount of drag simply because of that characteristic. Lighter lines also land on the water more softly, spooking trout less, so with them you can get away with using shorter leaders. Heavier lines are stiffer and won't flow or bend as well in the currents, an important consideration when fishing small flies.

Rods of all lengths and actions can be used for small fly fishing. In the cane rod days, shorter rods were preferred because longer rods were too heavy and noodley. Then, 6 to 7 1/2-foot rods were the standard. With the advent of fiberglass, rod length increased to an average of 8 to 8 1/2 feet. Now graphite technology has fostered the development of lightweight rods in a number of line weights in lengths of from 6 to 10 feet, and even longer. The general consensus today is that 8 1/2 to 9-footers are the most useful graphite rods for fishing most streams, as far as performance goes. The longer rods have more backbone, which yields better casting distance, better line-mending control, better performance in windy conditions, and more backbone for fighting larger fish.

But there are always exceptions. For example, on small, brushy streams where a long rod will become tangled in the brush, a 6 or 7-foot rod is obviously a better choice. Such shorter rods don't work well for casting for distance or into the wind, but often they rate high on the fun factor for small water. In line weights from 1 to 4, rods no longer than 8 1/2 feet are frequently preferred. The shorter rods weigh less and their feather-light weight makes them pleasant to cast all day.

Rods longer than 9 feet have become more popular as graphite rod design improves. The long rods can easily mend large amounts of line, can roll cast farther and can back cast over tall streamside brush. But their minuses include added cost and weight, and a whippy nature in the very light line sizes.

Rod action is very subjective. Many western anglers who fish large, windy rivers prefer a stiff casting action. Softer rods are preferred by others. The answer to rod selection is to cast the rod before you buy it. If it suits your casting style, then it's a good rod for you. My personal preference in rods for small flies is a 3-weight 8-footer for small dry flies, and a 4-weight 9-footer with a stiff action for all-around fishing. On lakes and larger streams where wind and casting distance is a factor, I'll go to a 6-weight 9-foot rod. I also have a 4-weight 6-footer for those small brushy streams.

Light rods suit the lighter tippets that are normally used in small fly fishing. A 3-weight rod with 5X-tippet and a well-tied knot is a tough rig for a trout to escape from if you are using good technique. You can put a surprising amount of pressure on a trout with such a light rod because of its shock-absorbing qualities. Actually, heavier rods are prone to break light tippets much more easily. A 6-weight rod can easily break 5X-tippet on the hook-set (unless you use a slip strike), and it does not give you as much flex during the fight for those sudden surges that trout are famous for.

Lines

Whether you are fishing small dry flies, nymphs, or emergers, floating lines are used for 90 percent of all stream fishing. They provide you with the best control over drift because they can be mended and adjusted easier than sinking lines. In lake fishing, floating lines are valuable for casting dry flies to cruisers, for fishing weighted nymphs slowly, and for presenting emergers.

Among floating lines, your basic choice is between a double-taper and a weight-forward taper. Double-taper floating lines are popular with dry-fly fishermen, particularly those using lighter line weights, as many have longer forward tapers (that are better for delicate casting) than do weight-forward lines.

Weight-forward floating lines are a better choice for larger rivers and lakes where distance casting is an advantage, because most people can achieve greater distance with a weight-forward than a double-taper. Actually, the newer commercial lines being manufactured today have double-taper and weight-forward designs that are quite similar in performance. Both are fine, so it's really a matter of personal choice.

Sinking lines are seldom used in streams, where most presentations are aimed at achieving a drag-free drift that can only be achieved with a floating line. Also, there are few sinking lines available today in the very light weights that you would be using for small fly fishing on streams. Some 4-weight sinking lines are on the market, but more commonly you will only see sinking lines in the range from 6-weight and heavier in fly shops.

For stream fishing, the principal use of a sinking line is for those situations that require that you make an active retrieve, such as streamer, leech, or crayfish presentations. For this work, depending upon the water depth and type of presentation you are trying to achieve, you can choose from a wide choice of sink-tip or full-sinking lines in a number of densities and sink rates.

If you are presenting small flies on a lake, however, sinking lines can make a big difference. Here you will likely be encountering fish at a number of levels in the water column. To fish each of these levels effectively, you may need several sinking lines of different densities and sink rates — from a slow-sinking line with neutral density (often referred to as an intermediate line) all the way up to progressively faster-sinking lines, designated as Types I through VI, with the very highest designation, a VI line, being an ultra-fast sinker.

Leaders

Leaders come in all lengths, sizes and tapers today. Some are designed with long, light tippets. Others are stiffer so that they will turn over better in the wind or when casting with large flies. Unfortunately, few manufacturers specify the taper style of their leaders, so you need to learn how to adapt the leaders you have purchased to the casting situations you will be encountering.

Tippet lengths vary greatly. Most commercial leaders have tippets from 2 to 5 feet long. A long tippet is designed to turn over poorly on purpose so that it will land in light coils and aid in presenting the fly naturally. This is an important tippet characteristic for trout that are very selective to natural drift.

If you have a drag problem, it may be partially solved just by lengthening the tippet. But in windy conditions, a long, light tippet gets blown all over the place and will work against you, and you will probably have to shorten it for more efficiency in the wind.

Adapting leaders is thus as simple as cutting out or lengthening leader sections as needed. You should carry a selection of tapered leaders and tippet sizes from 0X to 6X. A 7 1/2-foot, 4X-leader with an added 2 to 3 feet of lighter tippet material makes a good natural-drift leader without making the leader too long.

Leader length can vary considerably. Overall lengths of 7 1/2 to 15 feet are regularly used for small flies. The shorter leaders are used for fishing small streams and for uneducated trout. The longer leaders are used for super-selective trout in flat, clear water, or in lakes and ponds where you want the fly to sink on a floating line. Common overall leader lengths for small flies on floating lines are from 9 to 11 feet long. Sinking lines work best with 3 to 7-foot leaders.

Tippet size is a great cause for debate in some fly-fishing circles. Extremely light tippets from 7X to 9X allow a very good natural drift, but they are not strong enough to land a trout in a short enough time to keep from exhausting and possibly harming the fish. Also, trout oftentimes want to bury themselves under weedbeds during the fight, and with a light tippet you may not be able to put enough pressure on the trout to prevent it from doing that. And if the trout breaks you off in a weedbed, it may be so tired that it will not have the strength to extricate itself and will, consequently, die there.

My own philosophy is to use the heaviest tippet I can possibly get away with. This practice is for the trout's benefit. The fight is quicker, I land more big trout, and both the ones I land and those that break me off have a much better survival rate.

The 4X to 6X-tippet sizes are usually plenty strong for small flies if they are sufficiently limp to obtain a good drift and you have tied good knots. I have not used 7X or lighter tippets in years, and have not missed it, even with #24 flies. If I can get the tippet through the eye of the hook, that's good enough for me. As new tippet designs come along that have greater strength with less diameter, I may change my mind. But for now, I won't go below a 6X-tippet and seldom below 5X.

Small Fly Hooks

I do not think that enough attention has been given to small hook design in the past, but things are starting to change as demand for better products increase. Many varieties of small hooks are available today. By their nature, small hooks require their design to be good to insure proper tempering of the steel, sharp points, fine barbs, adequate gapes, strong bends, proper shank length and eye positioning.

Extra-fine hook wire floats best on dry flies, but it can easily bend out of shape if a large trout twists violently or powers away. Adequate wire size is needed to be matched with fish size and power. So if necessary, tie your small flies on heavier wire hooks or on a size larger hook than you would normally use.

The gape of the hook can make or break a small fly's effectiveness. Several hook designs now incorporate a wider gape or offset point for better hooking. Extremely small gapes have a hard time finding something to grab onto during the strike and can literally slip right through a trout's teeth. Gapes on #18 and smaller hooks can be improved by using a straight-eye hook. Down-eye hooks can block some of the critical gape, and up-eye hooks sometimes provide a poor hooking angle. My extensive observations on this matter have shown that on #18 or smaller hooks, straight-eye hooks with wide gapes and sharp points hook trout much better than standard down-eye versions. (Larger hooks are not as critical and down-eye hooks might actually improve hooking angles on larger hooks.)

Long-shank hooks are okay down to #18, but in any smaller size are self defeating and are rarely found in straight-eye hooks. Standard and short-shank hooks have wider gapes for the same body length. For example, a standard length for a #16 short-shank hook has about the same shank length (and fly body size) as a #18 or #20 long-shank hook. The wide-gape version of the #16 can double the hooking gape and increase hook-ups considerably over the #18 or #20 long-shank hooks, with the same actual fly body size. Do you see the point? The smaller the hook, the more critical the hook gape becomes, with wide-gape, short-shank, straight-eye hooks being the best performers.

Small Fly Pattern Design

The design of the fly pattern can also reduce or increase hook-up ratios. Small flies that are tied too bulky can reduce the hook gape sufficiently to prevent easy hooking. For easy hooking, small flies should be tied sparsely, with any bulky materials kept on top of the hook.

Stiff wings can also reduce hooking efficiency by twisting the hook away from the ideal hooking angle as the trout closes its mouth. Stiff hair wings on small Humpys or parachute patterns can therefore be detrimental. Crush the wings several times to soften them up or tie them with softer materials, such as Z-Lon, for the wings.

Long, stiff tails on small dry flies can have a similar effect. Soft tails on dry flies and nymphs not only help improve hooking but generally look more natural. I've gone to soft-hackle tails, such as partridge, on many of my smaller dry and nymph patterns.

INDEX